Haleakala:
A Guide to the Mountain

A majestic silversword *(Argyroxiphium sandwicense)*, five feet high and arising from bare cinders, is one of Haleakala's floral miracles.

by Cameron B. and Angela K. Kepler

Design by Angela K. Kepler

Mutual Publishing
Honolulu, Hawaii

1

Rare native lobelias and mosses dangle over a misty precipice in Waikamoi Preserve at 5,700 feet elevation.

Photo Credits
All photos by Angela K. and Cameron B. Kepler except the following (t =top, b=bottom, c=center, l=left, r=right): David Boynton p. 30, 34(b), 41(c), 61(b); John Carothers p. 34(c), 64(c), 77(b), 79(1b), 86(c); Department of Land & Natural Resources p. 28(t); DLNR/Douglas Pratt p. 71(b); Fern Duvall/ DLNR p. 17(b); Dann Espy/U.S. Fish & Wildlife Service p. 53(r); Haleakala National Park p. 25(t), 28(c), 31(t), 38(cl), 43(t), 72(b); Hugo Huntzinger p. 90(b1); John Jenkins p. 16(t); Warren King p. 28(b), 52(t); Jim Larson/ Haleakala National park p. 5, 44; Ronald Lester p. 25(b); Jacob Mau p. 16(c,b), 17(tl,tr), 23(c), 41(t,b), 66(t); Skinner Communications/Tedeschi Vineyards p. 26(c); Dick Veitch/New Zealand Wildlife Service p. 86(t); Robert Western p. 33, 34(t); Douglas Peebles front and back cover.

Printed in Japan

TABLE OF CONTENTS

Mauna Kea and Mauna Loa, shield volcanoes on the Island of Hawaii, float above a sea of clouds and jagged lava on Haleakala Crater's sidewalls.

Helicopter pilot Tom Hauptman braves inclement weather to pick up National Park Service volunteers in a remote greensword bog, 5,200 feet above Hana.

ACKNOWLEDGEMENTS

Over a period of eleven years, many people have contributed to the evolution of this book. We particularly wish to thank the personnel of Haleakala National Park for their cooperation, stimulation and friendship, especially Hugo Huntzinger, Ron Nagata, Lloyd Loope, Art Medeiros, Betsy Gagné, Carmelle Crivellone, Carol Beadle, Adele Fevella, Jim Boll and Ted Rodrigues. The Nature Conservancy, U.S. Fish & Wildlife Service, East Maui Irrigation Company, Hawaii Department of Land and Natural Resources, Sierra Club, State of Hawaii, Mauna Ala Hiking Club, and Haleakala, Hana, Kaupo, and Kaonoulu ranches also provided assistance ranging from granting land access to conducting endangered species research and public education.

There is a very special bond that develops during the sharing of hardships. All those who shared pouring rain, biting winds, scorching sun, precious droplets of water and morsels of squashed food; who fixed vehicles, checked our whereabouts with radios, or otherwise hiked with us, we sincerely thank for their company and knowledge: John Carothers, Derral Herbst, Bob Hobdy, Alan Holt, Jim Jacobi, Stephen Mountainspring, Peter and Bob Pyle, J. Michael Scott, Ted and Pam Simons and Kelvin Taketa are particularly notable.

Tom Hauptman of Pacific Helicopter Tours, Inc., a remarkable bush pilot, took us and our personal welfare under his wings (literally and metaphorically), frequently flying through thick fog and stormy winds to deliver us safely to our destinations. To other friends, colleagues, and business associates who expressed *aloha* to us, we extend our heartfelt thanks. Lastly, we express grateful thanks to all the photographers and organizations (listed in the Photo Credits) who allowed us to use their color slides, and to Sue Nakamura for drafting the maps.

PREFACE

Haleakala: "House of the Sun." Its lunar landscapes, sweeping volcanic panoramas, glorious sunrises and spectacular silverswords are splashed on practically every brochure that advertises the Hawaiian Islands. For some, the name recalls visions of multi-hued cinder cones resting deep within a cliff-girt crater, of titanic struggles between the Polynesian demi-god Maui and his adversary, the sun. Others think of long bicycle rides from its 10,000-foot summit to the sea, or of farms sending gorgeous flowers around the globe. A few may even imagine remote forests or splendid waterfalls providing water vital to Maui's economy. To many, it provides exhilarating hikes, or is a source of potent spiritual energy. A coveted destination, Haleakala attracts nearly one million tourists annually. What is this mountain?

To begin with, Haleakala rises nearly 30,000 feet from the ocean floor. More than 93 percent of its bulk lies beneath the waves — we actually see only the top third of its height. The mountain's relatively gentle slopes brand it as a young shield volcano, slightly less than a million years old. Fire, wind and water combined forces to mold its current shape. Today dormant, the mountain has aged uniquely and wondrously. Its cone-studded summit depression provides timeless, planetary vistas that have fascinated visitors for over a century. Equally impressive are its biological treasures. Haleakala's diverse habitats range from high barren deserts which receive less than ten inches of rain annually to grasslands, alpine shrublands, bogs of exquisite beauty and extremely wet rain forests which receive over 400 inches of rain annually. This multiplicity of life zones is equivalent to driving from Mexico to Alaska. It was this combination of physical beauty and impressive biological diversity that led to the creation of Haleakala National Park, and later to an International Biosphere Preserve. Early in the 19th century, farmers recognized Haleakala as a precious economic resource — her moist, mid-elevation *koa* forests, once cleared, would be ideal for cattle ranching and small-scale agriculture. Streams flowing from its north slope are still indispensable for much of Maui's domestic water supply and for irrigation of the island's principal crops, sugarcane and pineapple.

A rare winter snowscape along Sliding Sands Trail in 1966. Mauna Kea (Island of Hawaii) looms in the clear distance.

5

This comprehensive road and trail guide is divided into seven chapters, each corresponding to an area delineated in the maps (p. 8). It begins with Maui's upcountry region, then moves through Haleakala National Park's highly visited frontcountry and crater rim before jumping off into more and more remote areas. The area covered is the entire visible mass of Maui's major mountain. From sun-spangled shorelines through lush lowland forests, verdant pastures and alpine shrublands, we travel higher and higher till rocky precipices, fog-cloaked ridges, colorful cinder cones and sunbaked lunarscapes of grandiose beauty greet our eyes. The book covers a broad range of topics: accommodation; birds; camping; climate; conservation; ethnic heritage; hiking; flowers (native, introduced and commercial); geography; geology; history; and truck farming.

For many, Haleakala's cloud-filled crater is the "top of the world," literally and metaphorically. Let its palpable stillness and unique magic bathe you with its energizing power.

Ashby's banksia *(Banksia ashbyi)*, one of the dazzling proteas grown in upcountry Maui. It smells like buttered popcorn.

A blazing February sunset from the mid-slopes of Haleakala highlights the Island of Lanai (left), Maalaea Bay (center), and the West Maui Mountains (right).

A close relative of silverswords, a bog-loving greensword (*Argyroxiphium virescens*) blooms in glorious beauty amid constant mountain fog.

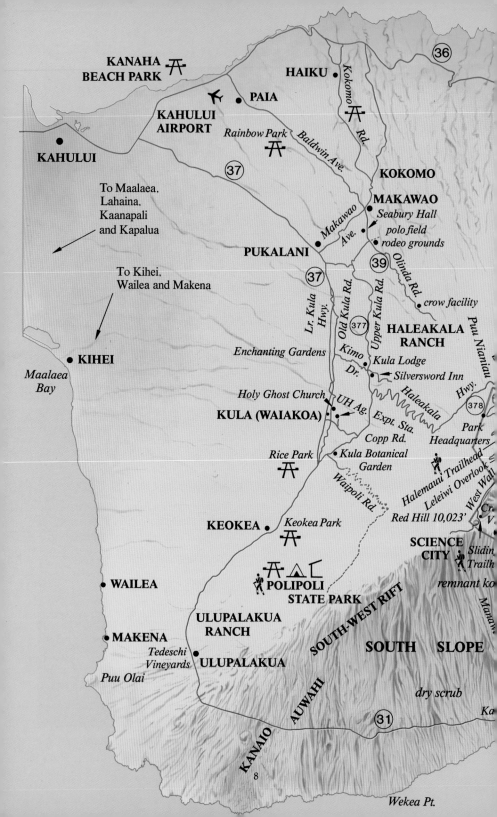

KANAHA
BEACH PARK ✈

HAIKU

PAIA

KAHULUI
AIRPORT

Rainbow Park

KAHULUI

36

Kokomo Rd.

Baldwin Ave.

KOKOMO

37

MAKAWAO

Seabury Hall
polo field
rodeo grounds

To Maalaea,
Lahaina,
Kaanapali
and Kapalua

Makawao Ave.

PUKALANI

39

Olinda Rd.

crow facility

To Kihei,
Wailea and Makena

37

Lr. Kula Hwy.

Old Kula Rd.

Upper Kula Rd.

377

HALEAKALA
RANCH

KIHEI

*Maalaea
Bay*

Enchanting Gardens

*Kimo
Dr.*

Kula Lodge
Silversword Inn

Puu Nianiau Hwy.

378

Holy Ghost Church

*UH Ag.
Expt. Sta.*

Haleakala

Park
Headquarters

KULA (WAIAKOA)

Copp Rd.

Rice Park ✈

*Kula Botanical
Garden*

Halemauu Trailhead
Leleiwi Overlook

West Wall

Waipoli Rd

Red Hill 10,023'

Cr.
V.

KEOKEA

Keokea Park ✈

SCIENCE
CITY

*Slidin.
Trailh.*

remnant ko

WAILEA

✈ POLIPOLI
STATE PARK

ULUPALAKUA
RANCH

SOUTH-WEST RIFT

SOUTH   SLOPE

MAKENA

*Tedeschi
Vineyards*

ULUPALAKUA

Puu Olai

KANAIO

AUWAHI

dry scrub

Ka

31

8

Wekea Pt.

Manaw.

LEGEND

- - - - Unimproved Road

Airport

Picnic

Cabin

Campsites

Hiker

PACIFIC OCEAN

N

*Keanae
Peninsula*

Maipuaena Str.

Str.

KOOLAU GAP

Nahiku coast

Hana Hwy.

36

Hanawi Str.

**NORTH
SLOPE**

**WAIKAMOI
PRESERVE**

Hanakauhi Pk. 8907'

wet forest

HANA

**PARK
BOUNDARY**

L. Waianapanapa

L. Waieleele

kou

North Wall

Kalapawili Ridge

**ALEAKALA
ATIONAL PARK**

Palikea Str.

KIPAHULU VALLEY

31

**HALEAKALA
CRATER**

8201'

*Kuiki Pk.
7553'*

**KAUPO
GAP**

uth Wall

Haleakala Pk.

Waaala Gulch

Kahalulu Gulch

Manawainui Str.

Wailua Falls

Makahiku Falls

KIPAHULU

**OHEO GULCH
(SEVEN POOLS)**

Lelekea Bay

**KAUPO
VILLAGE**

Kailio Pt.

Scale

0   1   2   3 miles

0   6000   12000 18000 feet

9

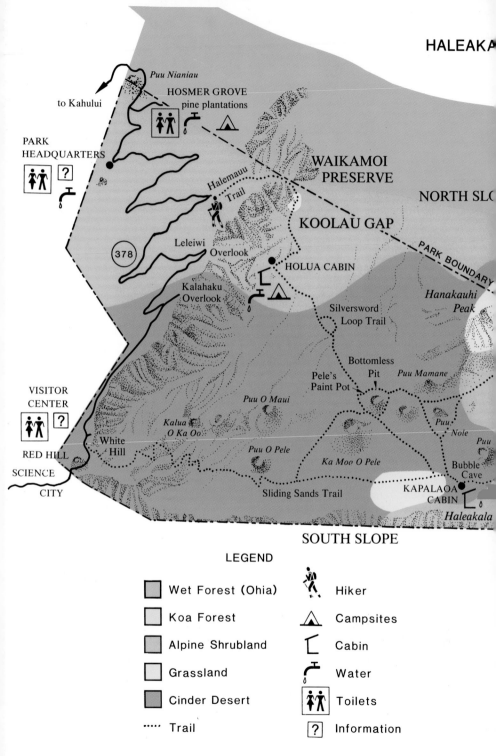

HALEAKA

to Kahului

Puu Nianiau

HOSMER GROVE
pine plantations

PARK
HEADQUARTERS

WAIKAMOI
PRESERVE

NORTH SL

378

Halemauu
Trail

KOOLAU GAP

PARK BOUNDARY

Leleiwi
Overlook

HOLUA CABIN

Kalahaku
Overlook

Silversword
Loop Trail

*Hanakauhi
Peak*

Bottomless
Pit

Puu Mamane

Pele's
Paint Pot

VISITOR
CENTER

Puu O Maui

Puu

Nole

*Kalua
O Ka Oo*

White
Hill

Puu O Pele

Puu

Ka Moo O Pele

Bubble
Cave

RED HILL

SCIENCE

CITY

Sliding Sands Trail

KAPALAOA
CABIN

Haleakala

SOUTH SLOPE

LEGEND

Wet Forest (Ohia)   Hiker

Koa Forest   Campsites

Alpine Shrubland   Cabin

Grassland   Water

Cinder Desert   Toilets

..... Trail   ? Information

10

I. UPCOUNTRY MAUI

Upcountry Maui. The name evokes mental images of a different type of island beauty: fields of proteas and carnations, "aerial" panoramas of Maui and adjacent islands, pastoral scenes, horse-riding and warm conversations around cozy fires.

"Upcountry" is a loosely defined region on Haleakala's broad western flank that contours south from Makawao and Olinda to Ulupalakua Ranch. Lying between about 1,500 and 4,000 feet, it is bounded below by sugarcane, pineapple and *kiawe*-dotted pastures; above, scattered towns probe upward against the fences of large cattle ranches.

Since temperature decreases about three degrees for each 1000-feet gain in elevation, the region is typically cool; many homes have well-used fireplaces, as nighttime temperatures in winter occasionally drop below 40°F. This "area apart" is decidedly not tropical, with a climate more in tune with coastal California. It is little wonder that such tropical plants as papayas, mangoes, plumerias and coconuts give way to temperate species such as azaleas, fuschias, jacarandas, proteas and cabbages. Kula's cool temperatures, well-drained volcanic soils, frequent cloud cover and gentle breezes have been responsible for turning much of her land into a vegetable garden for the state, and a world center for the commercial production of exotic proteas. Newcomers to Maui as well as *kamaaina* (old-timers), seeking relief from the heat and commotion far below, are joining the farmers and cowboys in this unique segment of Hawaii. In so doing, they are turning Kula, Pukalani, Olinda and Makawao into bedroom communities for businesses located down the hill.

PINCUSHIONS (*Leucospermum* species and hybrids), originally from South Africa, are the best known and loved of all proteas. Their bushes bear an abundance of elegant, glossy flowerheads, especially during the cooler months, so specialized they are composed primarily of reproductive parts! Given care, each bloom will last three to four weeks.

Maui's loveliest **PASTORAL VISTAS** greet us in Makawao. The northeast tradewinds cool as they rise against the northern flank of Haleakala, producing sodden clouds that discharge more than 300 inches of rain each year upon its forested slopes. Normally, this air is deflected westward, dropping the last of its moisture on Olinda, Makawao and Pukalani. Such consistent rainfall produces Maui's lushest forage. Here, horses graze in evening light while a large fraction of Haleakala Dairy's herd loafs on the slope beyond.

Although a heavily mechanized agribusiness, **PINEAPPLES** must still be harvested by hand. Because the plants bear sharp serrated leaves, field workers, mostly women, must be protected with padded clothing and goggles, in addition to hats and scarves which provide relief from the sun. Pineapples are placed on conveyer belts that carry them to waiting trucks. In 1985, crop sales exceeded $45 million for the County of Maui, which also includes Lanai, Molokai and the uninhabited island of Kahoolawe.

PUKALANI, a crossroads community, links Makawao, via Makawao Avenue, with Kula, via Route 37, and Haleakala National Park, via routes 377 and 378. Increasing numbers of "settlers" from the hot lowlands are discovering Pukalani's warm days, cool nights and tapering tradewinds, which provide just enough moisture to keep gardens and crops green without the consistent rains that soak Makawao and Olinda, only three miles distant. Thus, the town is gradually overgrowing its surrounding pineapple plantations. Nearly a million visitors annually pass through, seeking Haleakala Crater, never discovering the area's quiet restaurants and shops. Pukalani boasts the only upcountry golf course and traffic light, as well as several gas stations, which may be of great use if you are traveling up to Haleakala Crater. Check your gas gauge here, as gasoline is unavailable for the next three hours' drive, to Haleakala summit and back to Pukalani.

Puka is a commonly used Hawaiian word meaning "hole" or "space." *Lani* means "heaven." Thus, Pukalani means "gap in the heavens," perhaps referring to a consistent patch of blue sky that separates the tradewind clouds from the convection clouds that daily build up over Kula.

RAINBOWS are a recurrent delight along the wavering edges of Pukalani's tradewind clouds.

At a prominent copse of jacaranda trees one-half mile above Pukalani, Highway 37 turns south toward Kula and Ulupalakua. It is here at **PUKALANI JUNCTION** that travelers to Haleakala should veer left onto Highway 377, the shortest route to Haleakala's summit.

One of the joys of upcountry driving is the sense of space that you feel. Enjoy these **PASTURES**, their livestock and the expansive views to sea and summit. From here come Maui's fresh milk, eggs and much island-reared beef. The verdant stillness provides a palpable contrast to the more frenetic pace at Maui's coastal developments. Is it any wonder that many of Maui's *kamaaina* families prefer these slopes above all other island locations?

During the early 1800s, King Kamehameha III imported three Mexican cowboys to domesticate wild cattle. These *españoles* became known as *paniolos,* a name which continues today. Their Wild West tradition dominates the flavor of **MAKAWAO,** upcountry's unofficial capital. Makawao's somewhat dilapidated wooden storefronts have recently enjoyed a facelift which cleverly combines the flavors of cowboys and those attracted to alternative lifestyles. Oldtimers still remember the bustle of activity here during World War II, when nearby Kokomo served as a U.S. Marine Base.

A flowering jacaranda graces the entrance to the **MAKAWAO LIBRARY,** which brings the services of an excellent statewide library system to upcountry residents.

15

Two highly different sports have diverged from their genesis in the *paniolo* lifestyles of Maui's upcountry ranches. Both are taken very seriously by devoted followers. Members of the **MAUI POLO CLUB** (above) keep stables of ponies, play vigorous matches with other island teams and hold national meets, as seen in this 1984 Michelob Cup action in Makawao. Many players from Hawaii maintain high national ratings and play throughout the U.S. Much closer to their *paniolo* roots, **COWBOYS** (left) vie for honors in several rodeo events each year. The most prominent is the famous **FOURTH OF JULY CELEBRATION** in Makawao (below).

One weekend each summer, local artisans gather at Seabury Hall, on Olinda Road, one mile above Makawao, to create a lively **CRAFT FAIR** replete with live entertainment, food and a dazzling display of local creations. The beautifully landscaped grounds of this revered private school add to the ambience of this decidedly upcountry tradition.

Are those **WOODEN APPARITIONS,** artfully carved by Bruce Whitaker (above right), imploring craft patrons to take them home to share the vision that inspired their creation?

Nature produces works of art as well, many as rare as the finest paintings. Hawaii has suffered more bird extinctions than anywhere else on earth, and 29 additional species are extremely rare, such as this **HAWAIIAN CROW** *(Corvus hawaiiensis).* Known to the Hawaiians as *'alala,* in 1987 this raven-sized bird numbered less than five in the wild and only eight in captivity, down from thousands a few decades ago. The fate of this Big Island species now rests on efforts to breed the small captive flock at facilities built for it in Olinda by the Hawaii Division of Forestry and Wildlife, U.S. Fish & Wildlife Service and the Army Corps of Engineers.

Hawaii boasts clean air, a tropical latitude and grandiose mountains. Combined with the nearly constant tradewinds, this provides an ever-changing panorama of **BEAUTIFUL CLOUDS.** Watching them is a fascinating upcountry pursuit; in fact, everywhere on Maui, clear skies dominate one's visual horizons. Don't miss the extraordinary diversity of clouds as you drive below, through and above them on your trip to the crater. They are as much a part of Haleakala as its splendid natural setting.

LATE AFTERNOON LIGHT streaming through a jacaranda tree in Kula frames a silvery Maalaea Bay.

Upcountry's annual display of **JACA-RANDAS** *(Jacaranda mimosaefolia)* should not be missed. Roadsides and gardens, sparkling with masses of brilliant lavender bells, unfold their beauty from April to June. Originally from South America, jacarandas bloom particularly profusely in upcountry Maui and its Big Island climatic equivalent, the Waimea-Kamuela area.

FLOWER FARMS IN KULA

Pink, red, white, yellow, mauve and "peppermint"—every year approximately 35 million **CARNATIONS**, worth about $1.5 million, beautify Kula's slopes. Their bushes, arranged in neat rows on small farms, are tucked away beyond the main roads, although you can see some along routes 377 and 378. If you wish to buy carnations, it is best to order them beforehand by phone (consult the Yellow Pages under Flowers, wholesale). Two of the major outlets are Kula Sunrise and Paradise Flower Farms.

Another member of the cut flower industry is the **CHRYSANTHEMUM** which, like the carnation, appears in a variety of horticultural colors. Some farms lie close to Kula's "Enchanting Gardens" which specializes in carpets of bright flowers.

PROTEAS

Just as the Greek god Proteus was able to change himself into innumerable shapes, so evolved his floral namesakes, proteas. Since the 1960s, these delightful botanical curiosities, native to South Africa and Australia, have brought Maui to the forefront of international protea growing. Their dazzling array of shapes, sizes and textures includes furry pink powderpuffs, bursts of orange fireworks, fleecy "pinecones," silky balls of cerise sporting feathery eyelashes, looped corncobs, golden spiky acorns and even "stuffed animals" with curly fur. Their flowers range in size from a few millimeters across to dignified whoppers that top twelve inches in diameter.

Proteas (pron. *pro*-tee-uh, not pro-*tay*-uh) thrive in Kula's dry, Mediterranean-type climate, favoring elevations between 2,000 and 4,000 feet. Frequent cloud cover, cool evening temperatures, ample sunshine, slightly acidic soils, local mountain breezes and excellent natural drainage all contribute to their optimum growth. The winter blooming season of several prime species not only covers the holiday period from Thanksgiving to Easter, but provides flowers to the international market that are unavailable from elsewhere. Each year, Maui-grown proteas set new world standards for superiority, rivalling the beauty and perfection of flowers from their original habitats.

Gorgeous proteas from this multi-million dollar industry are readily available on Maui. Fresh or dried flowers may be ordered or bought from retail outlets such as The Protea Gift Shoppe and Sunrise Market (en route to the crater, on routes 377 and 378, respectively), Maui Plantation (Waikapu), or down-country florists. They are also available from individ-

As it matures, this handsome **ROCKET PINCUSHION** (*Leucospermum reflexum*) unfurls its curved "pins" (actually female parts) out and downward, revealing a succession of resplendent, fiery colors.

ual farms, some of which are easily accessible with free walk-through gardens. Examples are Upcountry Protea Farm (at the top of upper Kimo Drive, off Route 377), and Proteas of Hawaii. This last farm is located opposite the University of Hawaii Agricultural Experimental Station, a research facility whose gardens are open to the public, and which always has stunning protea displays as few flowers are cut. The Kula Botanical Garden (Route 377, south of the Crater turnoff) also has a delightful protea garden. It is always wise to phone farms ahead of time to check their hours.

Once described as "possibly the most spectacular flower in the world," the **KING PROTEA** *(Protea cynaroides)* is exquisitely regal in its size, color and symmetry. Prime flowerheads, each consisting of layers of silvery-pink ringing a central snowy dome, can top twelve inches in diameter, although seven inches is more typical. Many floral arrangements and boxed proteas from Maui are designed around king proteas.

Hundreds of protea flowerheads await grading and shipment in a **WORKING SHED** typical of those at Kula's many protea farms.

RASPBERRY FROST BANKSIA *(Banksia menziesii),* a native of Australia, is a rich burgundy color with silvery stripes. Banksias, a sub-group of proteas native to Australia, are characterized by their dense, spiky flowerheads exhibiting spiral, coiled or ribbed patterns. As they mature, yellow bands appear from below, indicating that their pollen is ready for dissemination. Approximately twenty species grow in Kula.

TRUCK FARMING IN KULA

Kula, an Hawaiian name which linguistically means "plain" (but climatically also means "cooler") has long been an important agricultural region of Maui. Even though the name "Waiakoa" is obsolete, it still replaces "Kula" on most maps. After Kula's native *koa* forests were cleared, Hawaiians grew vegetables here, trading them for lowland commodities such as fish, salt and *limu* (seaweed). During the early 19th century, farmers grew large quantities of Irish potatoes to feed hungry whalers berthed at Lahaina. Today Kula's produce is quite varied, centering around onions (the famous sweet Maui onion is actually a variety from Texas), lettuce and members of the cabbage family. Arable upcountry land is dotted with picturesque market gardens that provide a quiet contrast to the huge plantations of sugarcane and pineapple at lower elevations. Averaging fifteen acres in size, they produce three to four crops each year for Hawaii's hotels and supermarkets. Over 1.5 million gallons of water per day flow from Haleakala's north slope to maintain these gardens in a climate that receives less than 40 inches of rain annually. Such water demand, coupled with periodic droughts (this is the mountain's leeward slope) and county zoning, has allowed the upcountry area to retain its rural character despite increasing pressures to grow.

Many farms, like the **CABBAGE PATCH** shown here, are meticulously tended by Japanese-Americans, descendants of homesteaders who moved upcountry early this century. Cabbage is the only vegetable crop in which Hawaii is essentially self-sufficient. Twelve million pounds of cabbages poke their heads out of Kula's soils each year, four-fifths of the state's annual consumption.

The soils that provide year-round production for Kula's farmers work well for the backyard gardener. This nine-year-old is partly hidden by a huge black-seeded Simpson **LETTUCE** that she helped to grow. Many upcountry residents harvest a wide variety of temperate vegetables, thereby easing their dependence on expensive produce shipped to the islands via Honolulu.

Less than 150 upcountry acres produce more than 2 million pounds of **KULA ONIONS,** world-renowned for their extraordinary, succulent sweetness.

White and octagonal, **CHURCH OF THE HOLY GHOST** (1897), crowned with its dazzling corrugated roof and delicate steeple, is an instantly recognizable Kula landmark. The only upcountry structure easily visible from Kahului, it was built in 1897 to serve the spiritual needs of a growing community of Portuguese immigrants who settled here from the Azores, Portuguese islands 900 miles west of Lisbon. It is listed on the Hawaii Register of Historic Places. The gilded bas-reliefs and wooden altars were shipped from Europe. Every summer, a day is set aside in which the congregation provides a free *luau* meal to the public. Guests are also entertained at flea markets, food stalls and a livestock auction. Although various tales explain this festive day, it apparently stems from an oath made by parishioners in the Azores. During a prolonged drought, they vowed to God that they would feed their community if He brought rain. They prayed, and rain fell in abundance. Consequently, the original faithful, and their descendents in a new land, have annually kept this promise.

PRICKLY PEAR CACTUS, or *panini, (Opuntia megacantha)* occupies large areas in Kula. Though deliciously sweet and juicy, they must be handled with gloves and tongs, and thoroughly scrubbed before eating. In addition to its obvious spines, each fruit is covered with thousands of miniscule spiny hairs which will attach themselves tenaciously to your mouth, tongue and skin, ruining your next few days.

Kula has a delightful small-town atmosphere, exemplified by the friendly folk at **CALASA SERVICE.** Motorists have been stopping for gasoline at this Copp Road location just *mauka* (toward the mountains) of Route 37, past mile 12, since 1932. A diesel pump was added in 1982 because two patrons owned diesel cars! Don't be surprised to see regulars giving, or receiving, fruits, vegetables or freshly baked goods as they stop to "fill 'er up."

A unique, colorful Hawaiian tradition is the annual **MAY DAY CELEBRATION,** open to the public and held at all of Hawaii's public schools. Graduates dress up as Hawaiian princes and princesses (below), complete with leis made of each island's official flower. At left, Lauralei Royster is adorned with the *lokelani* rose, Maui's official flower, during Kula Elementary School's 1986 celebration. Pupils participate in group dancing and singing: if you've never seen kindergarteners in tiny muumuus singing "aloha songs," this is a grand opportunity.

Hawaii's **ETHNIC DIVERSITY** thrives upcountry. Here, Korean girls, decked out in traditional costumes, take a photo break after singing Korean songs for the congregation at St. John's Episcopal Church in Keokea.

California redwoods stretch into a typical afternoon fog (above) high above Kula in **POLIPOLI STATE PARK,** while cypresses accent an equally common upcountry sunset (left). This remote park, containing a mixture of native and introduced temperate zone plants, has an overnight cabin, a large redwood grove and many lovely trails which serve both hikers and hunters. This is Maui's best game bird hunting area, also providing feral pigs and goats. A four-wheel-drive vehicle is recommended to reach it: access is via Waipoli Road, off Route 377. Cabin use and trail maps may be secured at the Hawaii Department of Land and Natural Resources, Wailuku (808-244-4352).

Layered clouds and a sinking sun conspire to heighten the pastoral beauty of historic **ULUPALAKUA RANCH,** which straddles Haleakala's southwest rift zone and forms the southern boundary of the upcountry area. Fresh lava poured into the ocean from cinder cones near here during Maui's most recent eruption in 1790. Formerly known as Rose Ranch, on account of its beautiful rose garden (including *lokelani)*, Ulupalakua was frequently visited by Honolulu's King Kalakaua. Much sugar was grown here; remains of the mill can still be seen opposite the wine-tasting room.

Maui's noted wine-growing area is a 20-acre parcel of Ulupalakua Ranch's 18,000 acres, **TEDESCHI VINE-YARDS,** Hawaii's only winery. Following four years of trials with 140 varieties of grapes, the owners chose Carnelian, a hybrid of Cabernet Sauvignon, Carignane and Grenache. This premium red grape produces both red and sparkling white wines, which can be sampled, along with a unique pineapple wine (Maui Blanc), at the tasting room located on Route 31 several miles east of Keokea (follow Route 37). Built of lava rock in 1856, this attractive tasting room is a modernized jail. Recently, Maui Blanc christened its first ship, the *S.S. Maui,* in Seattle.

Far away from tourist haunts, the **KULA LODGE** (top left) and **SILVER-SWORD INN** (center), upcountry's only sources of accommodation, sit beside Route 377 amid pleasant countryside and scattered residences. They are located close to Route 378, the final turnoff to Haleakala Crater. Their coziness, large fireplaces and stunning views are well known, their food is excellent and year-round cool evening temperatures provide welcome respite from the heat of Maui's coastal hotels.

Cheering upcountry roadsides is *koali*, a native **MORNING GLORY** (*Ipomoea congesta*). It is closely related to the *pohuehue*, which sprawls luxuriantly over Maui's sandy beaches.

AUSTRALIAN EUCALYPTUS GROVES dot the pastures of Haleakala Ranch. Of the hundreds of species of eucalyptus trees, these blue gums (*Eucalyptus globulus*) are the most aromatic; essential oils from them are used in Vicks products. Open your car windows as you pass through the big grove at 4,000 feet elevation — the strong scent is fantastic, especially after rains or within softly enveloping mists.

These sprightly **GRAY FRANCOLINS** *(Francolinus pondicerianus)* from India are newcomers to Hawaii. Introduced as game birds in 1958, they prefer hot, dry scrublands, making themselves at home in abundance from Kihei to around 4,000 feet elevation in Ulupalakua and Kula. They greet each day with vigorous, penetrating calls, functioning as unrequested alarm clocks for many an upcountry resident. Gardeners must carefully consider their predilection for weed seeds and pesty insects against their fondness for strawberries and tender vegetable seedlings.

RING-NECKED PHEASANTS

(Phasianus colchicus) are Hawaii's *kamaaina* game birds, first brought to the islands in 1875. Avidly sought by Maui sportsmen, they abound particularly on the larger ranches and near Polipoli State Park. During the fall hunting season, don't be surprised to find armed men stalking them in their grassy habitats beside Route 378. Visitors wishing to learn more about sport hunting should contact the Hawaii Department of Land and Natural Resources in Wailuku (808-244-4352).

The *pueo* or native **HAWAIIAN SHORT-EARED OWL** *(Asio flammeus sandwichensis)* is unusual among its kind. No exclusive nocturnal recluse, this hunter seeks mice, rats, insects and small birds during broad daylight. Often seen soaring softly high above cliffs, or low over the pastures and shrublands of Haleakala, any hawk-like bird seen on Maui will be a *pueo*. Hawks do not occur here, and no other crow-sized, mottled brown birds soar. Pale, night-flying owls are barn owls *(Tyto alba)*.

Possibly one of the most rigorous running courses ever attempted is Maui's celebrated **RUN-TO-THE-SUN,** an annual summer event that begins at Kanaha Beach Park, close to Kahului airport, and ends at Haleakala's 10,000-foot summit. It takes about two hours to drive the 38 miles, a journey most people find hot and tiring even from a car seat. Marathoners, from Hawaii, the mainland, and foreign countries, vie to surpass the awe-inspiring record of *four hours, 45 minutes,* attained by Mauian Steve Sobaje in 1985. The average time for finishers is eight hours.

Dropping 10,000 feet in 38 miles, **BICYCLISTS** enjoy one of Maui's newer thrills. Starting on Haleakala's crater rim and stopping every twenty minutes, riders bathe in the mountain's full panorama. They twist through Haleakala National Park, green pastures, eucalyptus groves, upper Kula, Makawao and pineapple and cane fields before disembarking in Paia from what has been described as "the most fun you can have, fully clothed, on Maui." Adventurers are well outfitted for hazards of road and weather. Their bikes, too, are rugged and equipped with powerful brakes. Check tourist information or hotel activity centers for current schedules and rates. The trips, requiring about eight hours, include hotel pickup, food and a "chaperone" van in case of an emergency or fatigue.

Looking west from 8,500′ on the Haleakala Crater road; West Maui looms above a sea of clouds. The Island of Molokai lies in the far distance.

II. FRONTCOUNTRY

Civilization retreats as Route 378 twists ever upward along its sinuous course, passing for quite some time through the expansive grasslands of 20,000-acre Haleakala Ranch. Maui's coasts and lowlands gradually recede, dwarfed by the lofty panoramas which widen to lay bare the entire western half of Maui and its four closest islands. As you look out your car window, you can easily visualize an ancient geological scene, when Kahoolawe (left), Lanai (center), West Maui and Molokai (right) were interconnected. Mentally lower the water levels between the islands and you are left with an image of *Maui Nui* ("Big Maui"), a prehistoric island almost three times the size of present-day Maui.

If you wish to take pictures, stop now. Watch the clouds above and below you; between 5,000 and 7,000 feet elevation, you may well enter a thick band of swirling fog, especially if you are driving up in the afternoon —who knows if clear skies lie ahead? Turn on your car lights if the clouds are dense.

Just when you begin to wonder if you will ever see the crater, the sun will probably stream through the atmosphere's nebulous mantle, dissipating its last wispy tendrils into brilliant clarity. Is this Shangri-la?

The Haleakala National Park sign lies ahead. You are entering the park's "frontcountry," the final stretch of alpine and rocky expanses lying within Haleakala National Park, before reaching the mighty mountain's peak.

Dwarfing a lone hiker, a **RIVER OF VAPORIZED FLUFF** pours into Haleakala Crater through Koolau Gap, while Hanakauhi Peak looms darkly above. The tops of such clouds, generally reaching 7,000 feet, mark the transition between wet forests underneath, receiving up to 400 inches of rain per year, and the drier alpine shrublands and grasslands at higher elevations.

Haleakala rises to 10,023 feet. Even in the tropics, one needs to be prepared for cold weather. Every few years, an exceptional winter storm deposits several inches of **SNOW** on its summit, transforming harsh volcanic profiles into the soft winterscape captured in this 1971 photograph.

Popularly known by its Hawaiian name, **NENE** (pron. nay-nay), this Hawaiian Goose *(Nesochen sandvicensis)* is both Hawaii's State Bird and an endangered species. It is a biological curiosity among waterfowl, having lost much of its foot webbing as it evolved in response to a barren lava environment. Nearly exterminated earlier this century, captively bred birds were released on Maui in 1962. Several tame birds are on display at the Park Headquarters, and wild ones can often be seen there or a short way up the highway loafing among roadside grasses.

Camel of the plant world, Hawaii's unique **SILVERSWORD** is so efficient at surviving in its desert-like environment that it can afford to spend up to twenty years before sending up its sole flower stalk. Researchers are probing into its secrets of water retention in the hope of finding clues with practical application to the commercial world of agriculture. As the world's population increases, more and more foods need to be grown on arid, poorly watered lands.

Gateway to Haleakala National Park, **PUU NIANIAU**, framed by the basaltic walls of upper Waikamoi gulch, presides over a sea of clouds. The road to Hosmer Grove lies at its base.

This familiar **NATIONAL PARK SIGN** welcomes tens of thousands of people each month to the unique splendors of Haleakala's high country.

Just inside the park boundary, a road leads east (left) for a half-mile to **HOSMER GROVE**, an excellent stopping point for lunch and an easy stroll before or after viewing the beauty of Haleakala's summit, 3,500 feet above. The park provides picnic tables, chemical toilets, a self-guiding nature trail and a campground with no permits required. Hikers can fill their canteens with clean, cold water here. Eucalyptus from Australia mix with pines, junipers, cedars and spruce from around the world. These trees were introduced by forester Ralph Hosmer in 1910 during an experimental program to arrest erosion and establish a timber industry as grazing by domestic and feral animals, as well as man-induced fires, had denuded the slopes.

Hike the self-guiding loop trial for an excellent introduction to the biology of the frontcountry. A fine panorama of regenerating native shrubland extends *mauka* (upslope).

BIRDS

Hawaii's native birds have suffered catastrophic losses since man first set foot in the archipelago, around 400 A.D. More than sixty species have become extinct, and an additional 29 species are endangered, figures totalling over eighty percent of Hawaii's bird fauna! For comparison, the entire continent of North America has 31 endangered birds (Whooping Crane, California Condor, etc.). Hosmer Grove is the only area on Maui accessible by paved road where native forest birds can be seen: a ravine along the loop trail is a good spot to look for them. Watch for 'I'iwi, Apapane, Amakihi and Maui Creeper, as well as the introduced Japanese White-eye, Red-billed Leiothrix and Spotted Dove.

A deep red with black wings, the APAPANE (Himatione sanguinea) is a nectar feeder, sipping floral honey from 'ohi'a and mamane blossoms with red pompons and golden peas, respectively. Hawaii's most abundant native bird, it flits from flower to flower in the tops of trees uttering a variety of twitters and trills. Observant visitors to Hosmer Grove should have no trouble spotting this brightly colored bird, found only in Hawaii.

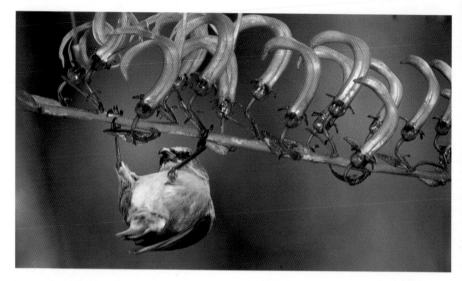

Less colorful than its nectar-sipping relatives, the omnivorous, yellow-green
AMAKIHI *(Hemignathus virens)* is a common forest bird.

Dazzling! No word better describes
the 'I'IWI *(Vestiaria coccinia)*. This
distinctive Hawaiian honeycreeper,
whose name is pronounced ee-ee-vee,
is less common than the *Apapane,* but
nonetheless conspicuous with its brilliant orange plumage, glossy black
wings and long curved beak.

An endearing little green bird with
a silvery ring around its eye, the
JAPANESE WHITE-EYE *(Zosterops
japonicus)* is a ubiquitous species
introduced to Hawaii in 1931 from
Japan. Highly successful and hardy,
it is now found from sea level to tree
line throughout the islands.

34

In this bird's eye view, a **CARPET OF NATIVE PLANTS** gleams in the brilliant sun, sweeping from the park boundary almost to the mountain's summit. This, the most extensive expanse of accessible alpine shrubland in Hawaii, houses a host of fascinating plants. The silvery patches are geraniums found only on Maui and the Island of Hawaii.

SILVER GERANIUMS (*Geranium cuneatum*), among the easiest native plants to identify, are especially common by the 8,000-foot parking lot at Halemauu Trailhead. From July to October, their low, rounded shrubs are bedecked with dainty white, five-petalled flowers measuring an inch across. Each shiny oval leaf is tipped with distinct "teeth." Do remember that it is illegal to pick flowers in a national park.

As the browsing pressure from feral goats is reduced through park management programs, Haleakala's **ALPINE SHRUBLANDS** are becoming taller and more diverse each year. Here, *mamane* and geraniums glow in the morning sun.

Haleakala Highway zigzags through the alpine shrubland of Haleakala's **FRONTCOUNTRY**, plugging forever upwards to the crater rim.

Golden flowers, long knobby seed-pods and lacy foliage characterize Hawaii's native **MAMANE** (*Sophora chrysophylla*), pronounced mah-mah-nee. Ancient Hawaiians utilized its durable yellow wood to make *o'o* (digging sticks), houseposts and one of their few recreational items, *holua* sleds, used for sliding down embankments. Like all Hawaii's native trees, *mamane* is an evergreen.

Every thirsty hiker in the crater has welcomed the colorful juiciness of a handful of **OHELO BERRIES** (*Vaccinium reticulatum*). One quickly develops an eye for the berries of a particular size, shape and skin thickness that are tastiest, even though they cannot compete with the delicacy and sweetness of their relatives, blueberries.

The park's most abundant shrub is the pink-berried **PUKIAWE** (*Styphelia tameiameiae*). Formerly used for elaborate *haku* leis, these quarter inch fruits are today an important source of food, not only for *Nene*, but for introduced game birds such as Ring-necked Pheasants. Most abundant in winter, they are not poisonous, as some believe, but neither are they juicy or tasty. Leave them for the birds.

Although nutritious for birds, the bright orange **PILO BERRIES** (*Coprosma montana*), common along park roads and trails, are inedible. They are related to coffee berries.

Captive *Nene* are kept next to the visitor center; others roam freely nearby. Even wild birds are inordinately tame, and several have been killed by cars, so please heed the **NENE SIGNS**, unique markers for an extraordinary bird.

One of the more common questions asked of park rangers is "Where are the restrooms?" Seek them at **PARK HEADQUARTERS**, Hosmer Grove, and Visitor Center at the crater rim. Park Headquarters, located three-quarters of a mile inside the park boundary, has much more to offer, however. Take time to enjoy the exhibits, silverswords, labelled native plants and captive *Nene*. Also available are brochures, books, maps, posters, film, abundant information, and ranger assistance. Those intending to camp in the crater, use the cabins (reservations should be made months in advance) or undertake extended hikes should register with the ranger. For after-hours' emergencies, contact the park staff by using the pay telephone near the living silversword display.

SANDALWOOD. Images of the past dance before our eyes: tranquil buddhas sit motionless as fragrant incense wafts around them, while Chinese artisans carve boxes of intricately inlaid woods. In Hawaii, we recall the rigorous slavery of thousands of natives, struggling on narrow mountain trails with heavy logs strapped to their backs. Their mission: to gather every scrap of sandalwood for the despotic chiefs to sell to crafty traders. This heart-rending period of island history decimated villages and forests, took Hawaii into the international world of trade and helped shape her future density. The several species of native sandalwoods are not extinct, as many people believe, but still exist in small numbers. This species, unique to the park *(Santalum haleakalae)* occurs along the highway close to Park Headquarters; one tree also grows on the right *(mauka)* near the dip on Hosmer Grove road.

CYCLISTS careen around Haleakala's rocky slopes above 9,000 feet. Behind them is the crater's precipitous lip. Close by to the right is the Park's Summit Visitor Center.

An introduced game bird from Eurasia, **CHUKAR** *(Alectoris chukar)* roams the rocky shrublands of Haleakala in flocks of eight to ten birds, often startling visitors by suddenly flushing in a burst of wings to flap frenetically off precipitous cliffs. Look for them along the road above 8,000 feet and at Kalahaku overlook.

EVENING PRIMROSE *(Oenothera stricta)*, a hardy alien from South America, thrives along road edges and trails, where its conspicuous sulphur-yellow flowers, blooming at night, erroneously suggest that it really belongs here. Hawaii has no native wildflowers in the conventional sense; any plant that looks like a wildflower was most likely introduced.

KUPAOA *(Raillardia menziesii)*, arising straight from dry cinders, cannot be missed, especially above 9,000 feet where it predominates. Even though it looks totally different from a silversword, these two plants are able to hybridize and produce viable offspring. This is such a strange alliance that biologists travel from near and far to witness this phenomenon, akin to a cross between an antelope and a pig!

The daisy-like flowers and leathery leaves of **KUPAOA** stand proudly erect against a bright alpine sky.

SILVERSWORDS

The silversword, Haleakala's "crown of jewels" and one of the plant wonders of the world, is a member of the enormous daisy family. Although the names Haleakala and silversword are normally linked, this striking plant's original range also encompassed three mountaintops on the Island of Hawaii. Today, due to extensive feral goat control in the park, the silversword is making a remarkable comeback from its endangered status; it now numbers over 50,000 plants. The ancient Hawaiians called it *ahinahina,* the name also applied to silver-gray hair. The common name derives from its Greek appelation, *Argyroxiphium sandwicense,* literally "silver sword of the Sandwich Islands" (the early English name for Hawaii).

A **SILVERSWORD** in full bloom arises from barren cinders which may heat to 140°F on scorching days. These gleaming, spheroid plants are able to draw on special water-retaining tissues, resembling clear green toothpaste, in their leaves.

Thick layers of white hairs on the silversword's leaves, together with trapped air, are responsible for their **FROSTY SHEEN.** This silvery covering shields the plant from the desiccating effects of sun and wind, additionally acting like a mirror to reflect away harmful ultraviolet radiation.

The silversword's **DAISY AFFINITIES** are unmistakable here. Flowering time is July through September.

Within the crater's desert-like environment, with loose cinders, strong winds, daily extremes of heat and cold, and precious little rain, it seems miraculous that a tiny seed can even germinate, let alone survive. Hikers beware: fifty percent of all **SEEDLING** mortality is due to trampling. Please stay on trails.

HALEAKALA CRATER

What an exhilarating experience! The stark cliffs below the Visitor Center drop precipitously to reveal a visual feast unsurpassed in Hawaii. The seven-mile long crater, into which the entire island of Manhattan could fit (heaven forbid!), resembles a landscape from a distant planet rather than from the earth. Yet who has not felt that here at last is "the top of the world"? Pocked with vivid, multi-hued cinder cones, the crater's cindery expanses sweep dramatically downward. Endlessly changing billows of cloud spill over windswept ridgetops or wander aimlessly amongst the upside-down volcanic bowls 3,000 feet below you. At times, these cinder cones resemble islands peeking above a misty sea. Far to the south, the massive Big Island peaks of Mauna Loa and Mauna Kea float on the distant skyline. It is easy to forget time and gaze for hours, especially when wandering clouds provide only tantalizing glimpses of the crater's beckoning expanses.

The remarkable crater (technically a caldera) before you is only 800,000 years old. The elemental forces of fire, water and wind combined to create, and continue to mold, this massive spectacle. At one time, Haleakala rose another 3,000 feet above its present rim. Torrential rains and thundering streams gouged the mountain, breaking through its sides to form two large canyons, Koolau (left) and Kaupo (far right). Subsequent lava flows, coursing downslope to the ocean, filled these two valleys. Although appearing small, the crater's cinder cones are impressive: Puu O Maui, the largest, rears 620 feet, or 70 stories high, above the crater floor.

Will future eruptions occur? Perhaps, for the volcano is really only sleeping; eruptions along its main southwest rift have occurred about once every century, although the last was in 1790. Permanence is an illusion; change inevitably controls every aspect of nature, including ourselves.

The **VIEW FROM THE PARK VISITOR CENTER** at Haleakala's summit, as you look to your left, includes the crater's west wall. Its oldest rocks are 800 thousand years old.

The ebb and flow of clouds, like tides on a beach, create an ever **FASCINATING PANORAMA** over Haleakala Crater.

DAWN AT HALEAKALA'S TOP-MOST VIEWPOINT: the sky's glowing colors seem to give us a fresh perspective on life. Each dawn becomes the beginning of time. The first non-Polynesians to experience the grandeur of Maui's highest peak were a group of New England missionaries in 1828.

Haleakala's sunrises are justifiably world-renowned. They are also very cold—frequently below freezing. Here huddled, **BLANKETED DAWN-WATCHERS** brave the elements as they anxiously await the first warming rays of a new day. To experience this awesome spectacle, be willing to sacrifice some sleep. Plan to reach Haleakala's summit a half-hour before sunrise, approximately 6:50 a.m. in winter; 5:50 in summer. Allow an additional two hours' driving time from Lahaina/Kaanapali or Kihei/Wailea areas, or one and one-half hours from Kahului/Wailuku. *Dress appropriately.* Temperatures can drop below freezing, and it is invariably windy. This is not the place for bikinis and *aloha* sportswear.

The year 1987 was the **"YEAR OF THE HAWAIIAN,"** beginning with a spiritual celebration at the top of Haleakala. For the entire year, festivals and cultural events were geared to recognition of Hawaiian contributions to the state's present well-being. Here a native Hawaiian walks regally in his *ti*-leaf raincoat.

MAUI SNARES THE SUN. Haleakala lies to the east of Wailuku, Kahului, Maalaea and Kihei, areas formerly inhibited by early Polynesians. At various times of year, the sun appears to rise directly from the mountain when viewed from these communities, and the massive volcano sends shadows over them long after the sun has brightened Hana. Perhaps for this reason the mountain was originally named *Haleakala*, "House of the Sun."

There is a well-known legend associated with this distinctive volcano. Maui, one of Polynesia's demigods, roamed the Pacific like a fabled Paul Bunyan. His numerous herculean exploits included "fishing up" New Zealand and the Hawaiian archipelago from the ocean. On the Island of Maui, Maui slowed the sun through treachery, although no one has yet explained to us why this didn't need doing in the thousands of years the Polynesians occupied other islands before arriving in Hawaii about 400 A.D. Perhaps because of our cooler sub-tropical climate, Hina, Maui's mother, was unable to dry her tapa during the short days here, and Maui, determined to help her, climbed Haleakala, snared the sun's long rays with strong rope, and bound the hapless captive to an *'ohi'a* tree. In the bargaining that followed, Maui agreed to release the sun if it promised to move more slowly across the sky so the tapa could dry. The pact concluded, Maui freed his captive, who ever since has moved at a more somber pace. Maui's epic struggle is here recreated by the late Paul Rockwood, whose striking painting graces the crater rim Visitor Center.

Hale-a-ka-la, House-of-the-Sun. Did it derive its name from Maui's exploits, or did Maui climb the mountain precisely because of its already well-known name? Did Maui's deed leave more than a legend here —his name perhaps? Alone among hundreds of islands settled by Polynesians, only one bears Maui's name. However derived, the names "Maui" and "Haleakala" are now bound more inseparably than ever Maui bound the sun, and together they continue to fascinate new arrivals to this land, much as Maui himself inspired a unique people scattered across a vast and tumultuous sea.

The sun, whose "official" home is Haleakala, occasionally forsakes the great mountain, yielding to high winds, fog, rain and even snow. Winter visitors, especially hikers, should always be prepared for fluctuating **CLIMATIC EXTREMES.** *Even if there is no snow, you should always carry a sweater or jacket to the summit, regardless of the time of day.*

A February storm creates a **SNOWSCAPE** of ephemeral beauty at the head of Sliding Sands Trail. Few indeed are the visitors privileged to witness the chilly stillness and magnificent gentleness of Haleakala in such a wintry mood.

SCIENCE CITY, sitting atop Haleakala's southwest rift adjacent to the park boundary, takes advantage of Hawaii's clear skies to probe the sun and track satellites. The complex also includes a variety of telecommunications facilities which relay messages between the islands.

HIKING IN HALEAKALA NATIONAL PARK

Haleakala may be appreciated from several fascinating perspectives. Most people stop only at the west rim Visitor Center near the summit, thereby depriving themselves of extraordinary vistas, unique plants and a deeper understanding of the park remote from crowds and only minutes from the road.

Whether you are planning short or extended hikes in Haleakala, please realize that the park embraces a wide range of climatic and topographic extremes. It is a mountainous wilderness complete with harsh weather; has rarified air, so go easy if you have a heart condition; is steep; and has crumbly cliffs, jagged lava and dense rain forest in the wetter areas. *Do not worry about snakes.* Hawaii has no native reptiles and only one small blind snake introduced from the Philippines, which is rarely seen. *Do not hike off the trails or travel alone, quietly give way to horses, and pack out all trash. Do not hike in flip-flops.* Dogs are prohibited to protect *Nene* and Dark-rumped Petrels. Pick up free information at park headquarters to help plan your trip. Call 808-572-7749 for park weather and 808-572-9306 for general information.

Leleiwi *pali* (cliff) is the best place in Hawaii to observe the **SPECTER OF THE BROCKEN,** a subtle full-circle rainbow around your own shadow projected onto clouds below you. If conditions are right, with a low western sun and abundant clouds slightly spilling over the cliff, the inspiration from this rare phenomenon is well worth the possible disappointment of a cloud-obscured vista.

SHORT FRONT-COUNTRY WALKS AND AREAS OF INTEREST

(For crater hikes see p. 47).

Hosmer Grove Nature Trail. Take Hosmer Road, 0.1 miles from the park entrance. This self-guiding nature trail is less than one mile long and requires about one hour.

Several **Crater Overlooks** are very rewarding, either alone or as part of ranger-guided interpretive walks during the summer—check the schedules at park headquarters.

1. *Halemauu Trail.* Beginning at the trailhead parking lot (7,990 feet, 4.4 miles from the park entrance), this two-mile round trip to the crater rim provides excellent views of alpine plants, the north slope and Koolau Gap. Allow two hours.

2. *Leleiwi Overlook.* Begin at the parking area inside the hairpin turn at 8,800 feet (7.2 miles from park entrance). Walk 200 yards (ten minutes) to the crater rim. Sheer cliffs, incredible views and a chance to see the Specter of the Brocken on misty afternoons (below).

3. *Kalahaku Overlook.* Park at 9,324 feet, at the end of Kalahaku Overlook Road. It is 8.6 miles from the park entrance. Access is restricted to cars returning from the summit. Climb up a few stairs and walk 100 feet to the crater view, or walk a short distance along a silversword interpretive trail.

4. *Crater Rim Visitor Center.* Park at 9,800 feet at the main Visitor Center, 10.4 miles from the park entrance. *The* destination for most park visitors, this area provides the preeminent crater view, a Visitor Center with exhibits, a small bookstore, toilets and the Sliding Sands Trailhead.

5. *White Hill.* Park at the Visitor Center. This easy 600-foot trail begins at the Visitor Center and takes you to the top of White Hill, a prominent basaltic knob with an outstanding view. It is excellent for energetic children.

6. *Puu Ulaula* (Red Hill). At 10,023 feet, 11.2 miles from the park entrance and capped by an enclosed exhibit building (see p. 41), this is Maui's highest point. There are excellent views of the crater, West Maui and the islands of Hawaii, Kahoolawe, Lanai and Molokai. Planted silverswords occupy the center of the parking area.

Nestled in the heart of alpine shrubland at 8,000 feet elevation, 4.4 miles past the park entrance, the **HALEMAUU TRAILHEAD** provides access to rare sandalwoods, brilliant silver geraniums and an extensive regenerating *mamane* forest. Its far-reaching panoramas, taking in many square miles of rain forest extending down to Maui's northern coasts, are splendid. Halemauu Trail traverses the mountain for approximately one mile at the crater rim at 7,600' then snakes down a steep cliff to the crater floor and Holua Cabin (4 miles) and continues on to Paliku Cabin, ten-plus miles and a world away. This is the principal route for hikers exiting the crater.

In this **RAIN FOREST** view from Halemauu Trail we see a spur ridge surmounted by the park's ambitious goat- and pig-control fence. Imagine constructing such a fence at a cost of nearly $100,000 per mile! Below lies the Nature Conservancy's Waikamoi Preserve.

LELEIWI PALI VIEW with clouds.

III. WESTERN CRATER FLOOR

Haleakala National Park. Most people are satisfied with the dramatic, top-of-the-world moonscape panorama from the Visitor Center, whose breathtaking beauty is generally enhanced by transitory cloud coverings. This is rewarding in its own right, and is all most visitors have time for—however, for those who wish to probe more deeply into the crater's secret recesses, there are more than thirty miles of well-maintained trails that will reward the hiker with unforgettable wilderness experiences. Perhaps, too, such adventures may uncover hitherto undiscovered facets of another precious wilderness—the human soul.

Because rainfall increases from 20" to more than 100" while travelling from west to east across the crater floor in a constantly changing topography, the hiker experiences many different worlds over short distances. The casual observer to the overlook cannot appreciate this. Such contrasts allow us to discuss the crater in two sections.

The *Western Crater Floor*, discussed here, includes the West Wall and upper Koolau Gap. This is the dry, colorful "moonscape" that has made Haleakala Crater famous. Best explored as part of two- or three-day hiking adventures, using tents or cabins for sleeping quarters, it may also be enjoyed by the energetic day hiker.

The *Eastern Crater Floor*, covering Paliku and Kaupo Gap, is discussed in the next chapter.

Revel in the crater's planetary beauty, clear starry skies, ethereal clouds, hushed solitude and palpable stillness. The more time and energy that you expend in your quest to soak up those ineffable qualities that constitute the very essence of Haleakala Crater, and that silently coax people back into its embrace, the greater will be your rewards. Your mind and spirit will draw on these precious experiences for years.

Photographic tips: Take light readings only from the ground. The sky and clouds at the crater are much brighter than you think. Include as little sky as possible in your photos. A wide-angle lens is useful.

Halemauu Trail winds westward past "Bottomless Pit" and Pele's Paint Pot amid the vivid colors of Haleakala's **CENTRAL CINDER CONES** *(puu)*.

46

CRATER HIKES

All crater hikes involve elevation changes exceeding 1,500 feet in rarified air approaching 10,000 feet. A long climb up late in the afternoon is characteristic. Hikers must anticipate the extra energy the exit climb will require. Crater trips are remarkably gratifying to those adequately prepared. The trail map (p. 10) will help plan your trip. Necessities, even for day hikes, include warm clothing (sweater, windbreaker, etc.), hat, good rain gear (garbage bags are inappropriate), sunglasses, lip balm, sunscreen, water, small first-aid kit, map, knife and small flashlight. *Campers, who must register at Park Headquarters before setting out,* should add a waterproof tent as Paliku is wet, extra clothes, and a cook kit with fuel; open fires are prohibited. *Those wishing cabins must reserve space three months in advance. Write or phone* Superintendent, Haleakala National Park, Box 369, Makawao, HI 96768; 808-572-9306. You will be informed of the sleeping arrangements at those times. A lottery system is used to allocate cabins. If you are unable to reserve a cabin ahead of time, you may be lucky to receive a cancelled one on short notice, especially if the weather is bad.

DAY TRIPS

1. **A Short Walk down Sliding Sands Trail.** Park your car at the Visitor Center parking lot at 9,800 feet. The trail parallels the last part of the summit road, on your right, then circles White Hill before descending into the crater to provide a constantly changing panorama of cinder cones, lava flows and crater walls. You can turn back at any point. Be aware of your energy reserves, as the return trip on the cindery trail is tiring.

Watch the clouds for indications of a sudden weather change. An entire day is needed to reach the crater floor and return to the Visitor Center.

Even one hour's **WALK BELOW THE CRATER RIM** provides an appreciation of Haleakala's grandeur — twenty-one miles of circumference and nineteen square miles of area — that cannot be gained from the Visitor Center overlook.

Hiking **SLIDING SANDS TRAIL** is like flying in slow motion: Haleakala's panorama unfolds gradually as you round White Hill and cross a saddle of gray cinders. First you glimpse the far wall of Paliku, seven and a half miles away, then the multicolored cones of cinder appear before you, their bases anchored in the plain below. This remarkable vista is constantly before you, framed by a multihued foreground and a perspective that changes as you descend. The first white men to venture into the crater were members of the U.S. Exploring Expedition in 1841.

2. **Sliding Sands Trail (9,780 feet) to Kalua O Ka Oo (8,200 feet): 5.0 miles, 4 hours round trip.** This is a variation on hike 1, following a spur trail to your left (2.5 miles) as you descend into the crater. *Kalua O Ka Oo* is an inordinately colorful *puu* whose yawning top is, uniquely, approached from above.

3. **Halemauu Trailhead (7,990 feet) to Holua cabin (6,960 feet): 7.8 miles, 6 hours round trip.** From the 8,000-foot parking lot (p. 45), the trail traverses one mile of alpine shrubland before reaching the crater rim at 7,600 feet, affording splendid views of Koolau Gap, Haleakala's north slope rain forests, and the north coast (with binoculars you may spot the Hana Highway far below). It then drops 1,000 feet in 1.9 miles of dramatic switchbacks etched into a sheer cliff (p. 49). The final mile crosses a meadow before surmounting an old lava flow to reach Holua Cabin (p. 55). A jagged lava tube *mauka* of the trail 100 yards east of the cabin can be traversed with a flashlight. Watch your step and your head!

4. **Sliding Sands Trail (9,780 feet) to Halemauu Trailhead (7,990 feet): 11.5 miles, 8–10 hours so allow an entire day.** This outstanding hike for the hardy combines the features of hikes 1 and 3, but adds the central *puu* (pp. 46, 47, 51), rock sculptures (p. 54), a cinder desert and the Silversword Loop (p. 54). Start early and carry food and water; a canteen refill is available behind Holua Cabin. The shortest route traverses the central craters on the *Ka Moa O Pele* trail (3.9 miles from the start). You end up six miles by road and 2,000 feet elevation below your starting point, so arrange for car pools, drop-offs at the summit, or pick-ups at Halemauu Trailhead. Many people camp the night before at Hosmer Grove (p. 32)

to assure an early morning start. Though extremely satisfying, this hike needs careful timing, so check sunrise and sunset times, remembering that at this latitude darkness generally falls before 7 p.m.

Sliding Sands Trail is the preferred route into Haleakala Crater because of its remarkable scenery and ease of access from the Visitor Center parking lot at 9,800 feet. It is not the best way out however, for its gradual 3,000 foot drop creates a tedious climb back, a difficulty magnified by thin air and loose cinders. For those on **HORSEBACK,** the trip out is easier, at least for the riders. Those wishing to see the crater by horseback should consult the Yellow Pages of Maui's phone book (under stables) or ask at Park Headquarters.

KALUA O KA OO, an easy stroll from Sliding Sands Trail, is in many ways the prettiest *puu* in the crater. Its colorful cinders barely push above the crater's flanks, while the west wall hovers above.

LELEIWI PALI, one of the crater's most exhilarating views, plunges 2,000 feet. Far below, rivers of lava lie frozen in their race to the sea, while Halemauu Trail visibly crosses Koolau Gap and surmounts the west wall in an impressive zig-zag, etched into sheer cliffs by the CCC workers over 50 years ago.

PUU O MAUI, the highest and most massive of all Haleakala's cinder cones, broods darkly 620 feet above the crater floor. Its impressive size, all but unnoticed from above, becomes increasingly apparent as one descends the trail.

Entering or exiting Haleakala Crater via the Halemauu Trail provides an impressive and somewhat enervating contrast to the relatively flat terrain of the crater floor. The trail, carved from basalt cliffs and wide enough for horses, affords spectacular views of Koolau Gap and the western crater floor. Photo shows the approach from Holua Cabin — note the wooden gate — and lower portion of **STEEP SWITCHBACKS.** Sweaty hikers always welcome the comforting afternoon mists that frequently hug the cliffs.

In sunny weather the crater can sizzle. Our favorite moods are during storms, when tantalizing mists part periodically, creating shadowy images that flicker briefly into one's consciousness, then dissipate into nothingness. The crater becomes a study in **SHADES OF GRAY.**

OVERNIGHT HIKES

Overnight hikes focus on the three visitor cabins—Kapalaoa, Paliku and Holua. All have fresh water (usually), chemical toilets and often a resident pair of *Nene* (pp. 31, 61). Designated campgrounds are near Holua and Paliku: campers should plan their trips around these sites. Help in emergencies may be sought at a back-country ranger cabin at Paliku (p. 61). Because of the multitude of hiking options within the interlocking crater trail system (see map, p. 10), we describe the routes to and from the cabins.

The most popular trips begin at Sliding Sands and exit via the Hale-mauu switchbacks, with a night at Paliku or Holua. An alternate crater exit is Kaupo Trail: a pick-up must be arranged.

1. **Sliding Sands (9,780 feet) to Kapalaoa Cabin (7,250 feet): 5.8 miles, an easy 3 hours.** This gloriously scenic, downhill trail offers a side trip to *Kalua O Ka Oo* (day trip 2). Just beyond *Ka Moa O Pele* junction (3.9 miles), where you continue straight ahead, the trail traverses a large grassy meadow (p. 51) before rounding a southern wall spur to arrive at Kapa-laoa. Paths to Halemauu Trail emanate from this dry area, ranging through a wonderland of cinder cones, silverswords, rock sculptures, a bubble cave (Puu Nole Trail) and Bottomless Pit.

2. **Kapalaoa (7,250 feet) to Paliku (6,380 feet): 3.7 miles, 2 hours.** Dry cinders yield to rough *aa* lava provid-ing footing for an alpine shrubland reminiscent of the "frontcountry." Sliding Sands Trail joins Halemauu Trail at Oili Puu at 6,646 feet, 2.4 miles east of Kapalaoa. Observe Mauna Loa and Mauna Kea framed by Kaupo Gap. A huge gravel outwash covered this junction in a 1980 storm,

a result of excessive browsing by feral goats which are now being controlled. Normally, a dense layer of misty rain greets the hiker, with rainfall increasing steadily down the final 1.3 miles to Paliku.

3. **Paliku (6,380 feet) to Kaupo Road (260 feet): 9.0 miles, 4 hours.** Beginning 0.3 miles west of Paliku, this rough track stretches unyieldingly down Kaupo Gap through a remnant *koa* forest (p. 64) before reaching the park boundary at 3,847 feet (3.5 miles). A hot, dusty trek through Kaupo Ranch takes you to Kaupo Road. Head 200 yards west (turn right) to find Kaupo Store (p. 65), a convenient rendezvous point. Don't yearn for a cold beer all the way down Haleakala, as chances are Kaupo Store will be closed. Cold beer/juice/water brought by a kind friend will be greatly appreciated. It is too far to hike from Paliku to Kipahulu camp-ground in one day (22 long, hot, dusty miles) and no drinking water is avail-able en route or at Kipahulu.

4. **Paliku Cabin Area** (see Chapter IV, p. 59). An easy hike takes you south through the Paliku pastures (p. 59) to an overview of Kaupo Gap. Enjoy the *'ohi'a* trees around Paliku and the *koa* in Kaupo Gap.

5. **Paliku (6,380 feet) to Holua (6,960 feet): 6.3 miles, 3-plus hours.** This terminal segment of Halemauu Trail is our favorite, for it encounters all that the crater offers except the overview. It begins in Paliku's wet *'ohi'a* grove, crossing a dry cinder desert to reach the alpine shrubland at Holua. Botanical specialties include a *mamane* forest, *Puu Mamane*, sil-verswords (pp. 31, 39), Maui worm-wood (p. 55) and rare lobelias (p. 56) on the cliff-faces behind Holua Cabin. There is rich humus, smooth *pahoehoe* and rough *aa* lavas, and deep cinders underfoot. Noted features include

Kalua Awa, spewing its frozen mass of black *aa* from the north wall (p. 60), lava dikes north of Puu Nole (p. 60), a 65-foot-deep "Bottomless Pit" and the vividly colored contours of Pele's Paint Pot (p. 53). Hike the Silversword Loop Trail — the extra 0.1 mile is amply repaid by close views of hundreds of Haleakala's famous silver rosettes (p. 54).

6. **Kapalaoa (7,250 feet) to Holua (6,960 feet): 3.8 miles, 2 hours by the shortest route.** Two trails, each dividing, cross the crater from the vicinity of Kapalaoa Cabin, joining Halemauu Trail in four places within 1.5 miles. We prefer the trail passing between Puu Nole, with its silversword mantle (right) and Puu Naue. It passes the Bubble Cave and joins Halemauu east of Bottomless Pit. Turn left (west) to reach Holua.

7. **Holua (6,960 feet) to Halemauu Trailhead (7,990 feet): 4.0 miles, 2 to 4 hours,** depending on your stamina. This is described in day trip 3 (p. 48): The bulk of one's time is spent climbing switchbacks.

Viewed from above, Haleakala Crater impresses observers with the grandiose scope of its alpine beauty. Inside, however, cinder cones dominate the horizon with their immensity and shapely symmetry. Here the flanks of **PUU NOLE** sprout a colony of regenerating silverswords whose sparkling silver rosettes contrast vibrantly with spattered lava strewn upon a cinder desert.

Amid the domination of volcanic features, a **GRASSLAND** can unexpectedly electrify the hiker. Shortly after Sliding Sands Trail reaches the crater floor, it passes through this broad meadow of native alpine tussock grass *(Deschampsia australis)*. Here a westering sun highlights its copious seeds, while behind a row of cinder cones steadily mounts the west wall.

51

DARK-RUMPED PETREL

The Dark-rumped Petrel or *'Ua'u* (pron. oo [as in goo]-ow [as in wow]) is an endangered seabird whose last substantial colony of about 400 pairs is in this park. Formerly abundant throughout the main Hawaiian Islands, this gray and white bird has been unable to withstand the depredations of rats, cats, dogs, mongooses, pigs and man. After living primarily on the open ocean, adults reclaim their earthen burrows in February-March and, after a brief honeymoon at sea, lay their eggs in April. The young are very slow to develop, leaving their cavernous homes after four months of darkness. Every year, Maui residents discover stunned birds around bright lights in the lowlands; the young fledge from their dark burrows and, attracted by the bright lights of tennis courts or football fields, fly toward them instead of out to sea.

Those wishing to see the petrels need the patience to listen for them at dusk, when they return from sea to tend their nests. Listen for their somewhat bloodcurdling yips, growls and groans. A prime spot is the Visitor Center from March to June. CAUTION: Stay behind the guard rails.

An adult **DARK-RUMPED PETREL** *(Pterodroma phaeopygia)* rests outside its burrow in Haleakala's west wall. These birds were eagerly trapped by ancient Hawaiians for food.

Biologist Ted Simons pauses beside an instrumented **PETREL BURROW**. His research led to management recommendations that are helping to augment the small population of this rare seabird.

This three-month-old downy **CHICK**, awaiting examination, will soon make its first nocturnal flight, unaided, to the sea.

Maui residents unwittingly threaten the existence of the Dark-rumped Petrel when they deposit unwanted **CATS** on Haleakala. Here the bleached bones and flea collar of someone's former pet provide testimony to a habit cruel to the animals, which rarely survive, and a danger to one of earth's threatened forms of life.

A lethal predator, a single **MONGOOSE** *(Herpestes auropunctatus)* will selectively locate one petrel burrow after another, destroying eggs, chicks and adults. Visitors can help the petrels by properly disposing of garbage so as not to attract mongooses and rats.

Fire and brimstone. Here the sensuous curves of **PELE'S PAINT POT,** Haleakala's most colorful setting, are splashed with earthy tones from the palate of Pele, Hawaii's goddess of fire. Sulfur produces the yellows, and iron oxides the rusty reds.

53

Large bombs tossed randomly upon a sea of cinders, phantom lava ships sailing upon congealed rivers of fire: the volcano reveals yet other moods. Such **LAVA SCULPTURES** assume a rich variety of shapes, sizes and shadows intriguing to the imaginative photographer, who willingly spends hours seeking a favorite fantasy among the contorted shapes. When hiking, pause to admire this unlikely feast, recalling the explosive forces that created it.

SILVERSWORDS are dramatically returning to former abundance along the short (0.1 mile) Silversword Loop Trail, located between Pele's Paint Pot and Holua Cabin. Here, visitors are led into the midst of the greatest concentration of accessible plants in the park. Please stay on the trail — *keiki* (seedling) silverswords are tiny (p. 39), easily overlooked and often crushed under the boots of a careless hiker. The silversword's fragile roots, as well as extending downward like carrots, also space themselves horizontally. In this way, both underground and surface water can be utilized.

As Halemauu Trail approaches Holua Cabin, the hiker is aware of changes underfoot. Loose cinders merge into *aa* (jagged) lava, the major product of cinder cones upslope. Numerous times lava coursed to the sea, and in places now exceeds 3,000 feet in depth. Over time, its numerous flows have filled much of the original streambed that gouged this huge gap in Haleakala's north wall. You can recognize this profile of the crater's **NORTH WALL** as the back side of the view you saw from the Visitor Center.

Three visitor cabins, dating from 1937, provide overnight shelter within Haleakala's summit depression. **HOLUA CABIN**, nestling close to Leleiwi Pali, has a good supply of potable water. Clouds from the north slope often extend up Koolau Gap, providing moisture that sustains Holua's lusher growth.

Lonely relics of a once abundant alpine species (goats love them), Maui's unique **WORMWOOD** *(Artemisia mauiensis)*is a sparkling white plant encountered on inaccessible ledges at high elevations; an excellent place is the steep portion of Halemauu Trail. This rounded shrub, with feathery, fragrant leaves, was named *hinahina-kuahiwi* ("silvery plant of the uplands") by the people of old, who used it to cure "mountain sickness."

Tall, stately and reminiscent of red-hot pokers (aloes), a native Hawaiian **LOBELIA** *(Lobelia grayana)* emerges from rocky outcrops near Holua Cabin. Notice the shining silvery undersides of its lance-shaped leaves and unusual curved purple-blue flowers.

Dotted here and there are prostate clumps of Hawaii's native **ALPINE TETRAMOLOPIUM** *(Tetramolopium humile)*, whose tiny, cheery daisies provide welcome relief from the crater's primarily barren terrain.

Only the hardiest of plants can survive in these high-elevation deserts, whose diurnal temperature fluctuations may exceed 70 degrees Fahrenheit. At left, the leathery **A'E FERN** *(Polypodium pellucidum)*, with large brown spore-cases clinging to the undersides of its leaves, creeps over a rocky precipice.

The attractive **CLIFFBRAKE** *(Pellaea ternifolia)* may not be recognized by everyone as a fern (right). Its clumped fronds, up to eight inches long and curled along their edges, typically emerge from shady crevices.

Ridges break steeply into **AINAHOU**, a circular section of Koolau Gap situated below the top of Halemauu's switchbacks and managed by the Nature Conservancy of Hawaii as part of its Waikamoi Preserve.

AMA'UMA'U FERN (*Sadleria cyatheoides*), common along the switchbacks, thrives in the daily mists that blanket this transition zone between wet forest and alpine shrubland. Its young, bronzy fronds contain a sunscreen which protects their growing tissues.

The verdant **AINAHOU CLIFFS** (left) contrast with the stark west face of **HANAKAUHI** (right), only two miles east, demonstrating extremes in weather, topography and vegetation found over short distances in the crater.

57

Biologists searching for Dark-rumped Petrel nests in Koolau Gap find a spectacular base camp among a jumble of **CRINKLY AA LAVA FLOWS.**

One of the authors (Cam) pauses — a **LONELY SENTINEL,** searching for a route down Koolau Gap's east wall.

In 1982, The Nature Conservancy of Hawaii acquired a conservation easement to 5,270 acres of lava fields, grasslands and forests adjoining Haleakala National Park's north boundary (Waikamoi Preserve), thereby augmenting the biological and visual protection of both areas through joint management. Pictured are the **WAIKAU AREA** (left), and **VERDANT 'OHI'A FORESTS** clothing Koolau Gap as it continues to the sea at Keanae Peninsula (right).

IV. EASTERN CRATER FLOOR: PALIKU AND KAUPO GAP

The most striking aspect of the crater's east end is its lushness. Gone are the barren expanses of cinders, the sparse shrubs on weathered lava. Suddenly, there are trees, succulent native raspberries and green pastures. East Maui is windward; clouds spill over the crater wall like massive Niagaras, bringing rainfall that often exceeds 200 inches per year. Campers must be equipped for rain and cold winds that haul down from the crater rim into an exposed campground. We once experienced 45 inches of rain in three days: dozens of thousand-foot waterfalls spilled over Paliku's precipices, roaring incessantly. A huge, swimmable lake temporarily replaced the pasture. Such profligate abundance of moisture allows the rain forest, which is typical of Haleakala's outer slopes, to creep tentatively over its rim into the crater.

Paliku is reached from the trailheads at Sliding Sands (9.5 miles) or Halemauu (10.2 miles). A downhill trail leads out Kaupo Gap to Kaupo Village (8.7 miles). For further information on trails see map (p. 10) and page 50.

MISTY ESCARPMENTS rise nearly 1,000 feet above the cabins (center distance) at Paliku.

A fenced **MEADOW** and lush grass contain park service and private horses at the base of Paliku's forested palisades.

Paliku is an older section of the summit depression spared from more recent lava flows which encroached from the west. In these **VIEWS FROM THE NORTH** (left) **AND SOUTH** (right), note how lavas streamed out Kaupo Gap, missing the eastern corner of the crater.

Hot magma extruded upward through cracks, hardened in place, then became exposed by erosion. These pillared **LAVA DIKES** along Halemauu Trail recount geological tales of searing heat and incredible pressures which fractured the old mountain.

Resembling a crumbling castle, the ruins of **KALUA AWA** ("channeled pit") provide rough footing for today's hikers. Note how copious flows of dark lava spilled out from this long-extinct volcanic *puu* situated at 7,500 feet on Haleakala Crater's northern flanks.

SLIDING SANDS TRAIL pierces a carpet of alpine shrubs as it heads towards Paliku, barely visible two miles ahead.

Paliku sports two cabins, a visitor cabin like those at Holua and Kapalaoa, and this **BACKCOUNTRY RANGER CABIN,** nestled beneath *'ohi'a* trees. Basic cabin supplies are delivered via horseback; however, firewood comes in by helicopter. Cooking facilities, bunks, eating utensils, firewood and sparkling water are provided. Bring your own sleeping bag.

MIST envelopes Paliku on most days, producing muted landscapes in addition to wet tents and clothes.

NENE PENS, on the edge of Paliku meadow, until 1985 marked the site of Maui's first (June 1962) and many subsequent releases of captively reared birds to the wild. This native wild goose is further described on page 31.

Dew-spangled, floral powderpuffs dot the **'OHI'A TREES** *(Metrosideros collina)* around Paliku, imparting a taste of the rain-soaked environments close by but unreachable. *'Ohi'a,* dominating all of Hawaii's mountain forests, were considered so sacred in ancient Hawaii that felling them without permission resulted in severe punishment, even death. They provide life-giving nectar and insects for native birds *(Apapane, 'I'iwi* and *Amakihi),* which often flit among their rounded foliage at Paliku.

Like a giant green shuttlecock, the ever-unfolding fronds of this native **WOODFERN,** *laukahi (Dryopteris wallichiana),* mingles with other lacy verdure in this moisture-laden corner of the mountain.

Hawaii's giant native raspberry, the **'AKALA** *(Rubus hawaiiensis)* is a welcome treat after a hot hike across the crater, although not quite as sweet as you might wish. Its summer ripening berries are best honeyed and cooked into a quick jam for your Paliku breakfast. This hardy perennial often colonizes sunny forest clearings; stay clear of its prickly stems.

The *'ulei,* or **HAWAIIAN HAW-THORNE** *(Osteomeles anthyllidifolia),* a native viny member of the rose family, flourishes among dryland shrubbery along the Kaupo Trail. Its flexible pink wood was used in old Hawaii for creative crafts such as toy bows and arrows (for shooting rats) and fishnet hoops, while its purple berries yielded a mauve dye.

MAUNA LOA and **MAUNA KEA**, on the Island of Hawaii, float above Kaupo Gap during early morning light. One million years ago, Haleakala resembled these behemoths in size, height (13,000 to 14,000 feet) and shape; rivers cut deeply into the mountain, just as streams are working now on younger Mauna Kea. The Hawaiian Islands are geologically ephemeral, each surviving a mere 15,000,000 years above the waves.

Streaming down Kaupo's eastern precipices (to your left as you hike down from the crater), **WATERFALLS** and/or billows of clouds create endless beauty while simultaneously widening the gap.

KOA! The largest trees in old Hawaii were *koa (Acacia koa),* and from them the grandest seafaring canoes were hewn. *Koa* is a legume, rich in nutrients, hence a favorite food of introduced mammals such as goats, sheep, cows and deer. It thrives naturally on mid-elevation slopes with moderate rainfall, conditions that are also excellent for ranching. Its superb wood, replete with rich variegated colors and swirling grains, is much sought after. As a result, *koa* is scarce. Some small groves cling to life in Kaupo Gap (below), showing signs of expansion now that goats are

under control. Hopefully, *koa* forests, with their associated plant and animal communities, will again crowd the entire length of Kaupo's side walls.

Living fossils, relics from 335 million years ago, when land animals first appeared on earth, **MOA** *(Psilotum nudum)* resembles clumps of tiny whisk brooms. Ancient Hawaiians gathered this insignificant, though not rare, little relative of ferns for a most unusual reason. A man's typical attire was a loincloth *(malo)* made from bark cloth (tapa) which, being rather coarse, rubbed against his tender loins. Gathered in quantity, the *moa's* yellow spore-cases provided a silky, saffron colored talcum powder that prevented chafing!

Seen from below, the geology of **KAUPO GAP** is vividly clear. The original Kaupo Stream lies buried under an awesome mass of lava thousands of feet thick. The flows plunged into the sea and spread out, forming a huge fan now occupied by Kaupo Ranch. In this late afternoon photo, clouds from Kipahulu Valley and Kuiki Peak, at 7,553 feet, characteristically pour over Kaupo Gap's eastern wall (center right).

Trail's end for many a hiker, the parking lot at **KAUPO STORE** marks the unofficial terminus of the long trek from the Visitor Center. The trail crosses private land beyond the park boundary, so please respect the rights of property owners. The entire village reminds us of old Hawaii, when the pace of living was considerably slower. Don't get excited about a cold beer as you hike . . . Kaupo store may well greet you with locked doors (right). We hope you've arranged for a friend to pick you up here (see p. 50)! To find the store, hike west (turn right) a short 200 yards when you reach Kaupo Road.

The happy faces of these **HAWAIIAN CHILDREN** reflect the easygoing way of life in this isolated, tight community. School is a long commute—either to Hana or Kula depending on road conditions. The bus to Kula leaves at 5:30 a.m.

A LATE AFTERNOON GLOW on the grazing lands of Kaupo Ranch illuminates arid scrub and the distant Island of Kahoolawe.

KAUPO CHURCH comes alive with local Hawaiians on Sundays.

V. HALEAKALA'S SOUTH SLOPE

Haleakala's south slope is remote and difficult of access. It is best seen out the right side of a commercial airplane flying between the Island of Hawaii and Maui. Closer in, flight-seeing excursions sometimes overfly its deeply eroded, barren landscape (below, right). Most tours avoid it, and rental cars are prohibited from driving its rough weather-beaten road, often closed due to landslides. To the true, down-home local, this area is known as "behind the mountain."

Extensive forests once joined Haleakala's north slope forests on both ends to clothe almost the entire mountain. *Koa* was king. Sadly, these forests are the most severely altered life zone on Maui, with only remnant patches attesting to their former grandeur. Those who do drive the Kaupo Road (Route 31) see only its fringes, where cattle graze (below, left) and little of its original nature remains for the untrained eye. In this book, the higher elevations of Haleakala's south slope are highlighted; for the Kaupo Road itself, see *Maui's Hana Highway: A Visitor's Guide,* and for its picturesque coastline, *Guide to South Maui: Kihei, Wailea, Molokini, Makena,* both by Angela Kay Kepler.

An aerial view of Haleakala's **SOUTH SLOPE**, showing Kaupo Gap on the left and the complex drainage patterns of Waoala and Kahalulu gulches.

A typical scene along the Kaupo Road looking up 9,000 feet to Haleakala's south rim via **PAHIHI GULCH**.

The bumpy skyline of Haleakala's southwest rift, wreathed in afternoon clouds and shadow, forms the western terminus of the **SOUTH SLOPE.** This abrupt turn in the mountain, corresponding to Ulupalakua, extends the crater's line of cinder cones from Science City to Makena and the offshore islands of Molokini and Kahoolawe. In 1778 Captain Cook witnessed a similar scene, simply stating that Haleakala was an "elevated hill . . . whose summit rose above the clouds."

Jumbled hillocks of crumbly, rusty-red lavas characterize the **SOUTHWEST RIFT.** Occasionally, the Sierra Club conducts hikes into this remote corner of Haleakala, arranging for pickups at the trail's end, Polipoli State Park in Kula.

A **DRY, CINDERY GULLY** below Red Hill's 10,023 foot height is continuously molded by alpine winds and infrequent winter storms.

Hana-side of Kaupo Gap, **MANA-WAINUI STREAM** plunges 1,600 feet into a large amphitheatre of its own creation. Strong updrafts generate an "upside-down falls." The nibblings of goats have opened up this remote *koa* forest and greatly accelerated its erosion.

The ancient Hawaiians must have liked the word *manawainui,* meaning "spirit of the big waters," as they used this name for two major gulches close to one another on Haleakala's south slope, and for another deep valley in West Maui. Kaupo Road crosses this **MANAWAINUI GULCH,** west of Kaupo Gap, near the coast.

An exceptionally clear day finds park biologists surveying heavily damaged alpine shrubland (compare with page 35) above Kaupo Gap. Jutting squarely into the sea is **KAILIO POINT,** a southern counterpart of Keanae Peninsula, a picturesque lava point passed on Maui's north coast Hana Highway. Both were formed from lavas coursing down large valleys into the ocean. Mauna Kea (left) and Mauna Loa (right) rise loftily above the omnipresent clouds.

The jumbled mass of sculpted basalt at **WEKEA POINT** reveals the salient characteristics of Maui's leeward coasts. Protected by the bulk of Haleakala from the north shore's heavy surf, and far less water-eroded because of lower rainfall, this shoreline lacks high cliffs and beaches. Its treacherously rocky shore caused much consternation to early explorers seeking safe landings for their ships.

Two centuries of heavy grazing by cattle, and browsing by goats, have reduced a once lush forest to tattered patches. Here, a **DYING TREEFERN** (*hapu'u*) indicates the loss of former life-giving shade trees.

This rare **AUWAHI SANDALWOOD** (*Santalum freycinetianum auwahiense*), different from the Haleakala Sandalwood (page 37), is unique to this area of Maui.

FOSSILS

Helen James systematically excavates a cavernous subterranean passageway, **NAIO TUBE.**

Recently, an exciting new chapter in Maui's biological history began to unfold. It began with the discovery of several large underground tunnels, former lava tubes, which contained unusually shaped bones. So significant were these finds that two world authorities on fossil birds, Storrs Olson and Helen James of the Smithsonian Institution, Washington, D.C., began extensive excavations. Layer upon layer of powdery soil unearthed skeletons from dozens of now-vanished species of birds, many of which had never been seen by white men, let alone described scientifically. Included were three foot-high, flightless geese and ibises, and numerous small Hawaiian honeycreepers. Excavations from other islands revealed extinct crows, owls and other exciting finds. This remarkable fossil material, dating back 10,000 years, also included bird species currently endangered on Maui and others known only from 19th century museum collections.

Haleakala's south slope was evidently once brimming with bird life, some of which became trapped in lava tubes, chronicling the events of thousands of years in this poignant manner.

UPPER AUWAHI CAVE repeats the above tale, reported to a surprised world in 1982. Here, skeletal material was so densely packed that in places investigators sifted through piles of bones barely separated by soil.

FLIGHTLESS BIRDS (ibis and rail) feed side by side in Douglas Pratt's rendition of an early Hawaiian landscape.

The Hawaiians built settlements all along Haleakala's south coast, as evidenced at **KANAIO,** a few miles east of Makena. Former wells associated with these village sites are now dry or brackish, indicating a loss of forest cover upslope, and are no longer capable of supporting human life.

During ancient times, Hawaiian men sometimes ventured up to high elevations on Haleakala, sheltering in **CAVES** such as this one at 7,000 feet elevation. Found only a few years ago, this cave, large enough to accommodate two people, contained *kukui* nuts for light, *opihi* (limpet) shells and Dark-rumped Petrel bones for food. Open sleeping shelters, *heiau* (temples), trails and other Polynesian relics are scattered on the upper south slopes and on into the crater.

GOATS roam Haleakala's south slope by the thousands. Their voracious nibbling has done more to turn native dry forests into wasteland than any other force in Hawaii. Although winsome, goats can survive only by munching on plant communities already endangered by their depredation.

Soil **"EROSION MUSHROOMS,"** up to five feet tall, are common in goat-ridden wastelands, graphically measuring former soil levels. In many areas, all the topsoil has disappeared, turning alpine shrublands into stony deserts.

Constructed in 1984, Haleakala National Park's **SOUTH BOUNDARY FENCE** (above and below) allows resource managers to protect its native plant communities from goats by preventing the constant immigration of thousands of animals that roam outside it. But who will protect the resources outside the fence?

VI. WET FORESTS

Highlighted by filtered yellow-green light, **MOSSES AND FERNS** exemplify the delicate beauty of Maui's rain forests.

Wet forests stretch from Haiku to Kipahulu, garlanding Haleakala's windward slopes with hundreds of species of plants and animals, many endangered and found nowhere else on earth. Receiving up to 400 inches of rain annually, the soggy terrain has been dissected by hundreds of gulches. Seemingly protected by their remoteness in this extremely rugged *de facto* wilderness area, these forests are actually under continuous assault by feral pigs, carnivorous snails, a host of alien weeds, and diseases that decimate native birds. Fortunately, steps are under way to protect the wealth of unique beauty chronicled in the following pages.

'OHI'A trees spend much of their time bathed in mist and rain, which must account for the Hawaiian belief, still held today, that picking its scarlet flowers will bring inclement weather. Native birds (pp. 33, 34) gain a large measure of their sustenance from this ubiquitous forest tree.

A typical **MIST-SHROUDED RAIN FOREST** scene high above Nahiku.

Unnamed **WATERFALLS** in abundance — cascades, falls and ribbons — splash into plunge pools and gorges as their streams, continuously fed by rain, race to the ocean. At 6,000 feet elevation there are 25 gulches along every mile of contour, posing considerable topographical inconvenience for the cross-country hiker.

Hawaii's native lobelias are a showcase for evolution: woody candelabras, palm-like shrubs and silversword-like rosettes brighten her pristine greenery (left). Many specialize in unusual textures: knobs, warts, spines, etc. The **PRICKLY CYANEA** *(Cyanea horrida)* displays its armor-coated flowers, stems and leaves (above).

Dusk reveals a meandering **RIVER OF CLOUDS** lapping against the north slope of Haleakala at 7,000 feet, marking timberline. Like aquatic vegetation at a river's edge, forest plants only tentatively extend above the temperature inversion layer that holds the clouds in place.

On rare days the clouds part, revealing an awe-inspiring carpet of green — alpine shrubs and rain forest — sweeping down towards the **NAHIKU COAST.** Though only six miles distant, the Hana Highway is three day's rugged hiking away.

SCIENTISTS IN RAIN GEAR add perspective to forests above 6,000 feet, where trees rarely exceed forty feet in height. Sideways movement across the mountain is slow — about one mile per day.

An aerial view of Kapia stream, **WAIHO VALLEY,** which sweeps from Haleakala Crater towards Hana.

In 1973, university students discovered a new species of bird, the **PO'O-ULI** *(Melamprosops phaeosoma),* one of the rarest birds in the world. Its entire geographic range is two square miles of low, tangled forest high above Nahiku (insert). Here, artist Patrick Ching depicts an adult feeding its mate at the first nest ever discovered (1986).

The perky personality of Maui's **CRESTED HONEYCREEPER** *(Palmeria dolei)* dominates all other birds as it flits from flower to flower high in the forest canopy. Although endangered, more than 3,000 individuals still seek food from Waikamoi to Kipahulu, and are occasionally seen at Hosmer Grove (p. 32).

These fuzzy black flowers, of a color seldom seen in nature, belong to a very rare lobelia, the **BLACK-FLOWERED CYANEA** *(Cyanea atra)*, unique to Maui.

The **PRICKLY-FLOWERED CYANEA,** or *haha (Cyanea aculeatiflora)*, is another gorgeous rare lobelia, restricted to a tiny patch of East Maui.

The **MOUNTAIN NAUPAKA** *(Scaevola chamissoniana)*, covered with appealing "half-flowers," is the upland relative of the succulent shrub that sprawls over many of Maui's beaches, the beach naupaka. This shrub is immortalized in Hawaiian legend as part of a poignant love story (see *Guide to South Maui*, by A. K. Kepler).

A LO'ULU FAN PALM *(Pritchardia arecina)*, unique to East Maui, is always a thrill to encounter. Formerly, the durable fronds of these palms were woven into sun-shades, fans, baskets and rain protectors *(lo'ulu* means "umbrella"). Their large tasty seeds are, unfortunately, eagerly devoured by feral pigs and rats, endangering the species' existence.

Clusters of long tubular flowers draw one's attention to this beautiful native vine, **KAMEHAMEHA'S MINT** *(Stenogyne kamehamehae)*, whose name commemorates the famous series of Hawaiian kings. Vines such as this attract flocks of native birds (p. 34).

Bursting with dainty blossoms, the **LARGE-LEAVED HALEAKALA GERANIUM** *(Geranium multiflorum)* is only found near timberline on Haleakala's north slope.

Within Haleakala National Park alone, 128 species and varieties of **MOSSES** have been identified. Their variety is staggering, from skinny tendrils streaming from branches to miniature umbrellas.

FERNS

What would a rain forest be like without ferns? From lacy maidenhairs to forty-foot-tall treeferns, Hawaii's 176 species of ferns impart a delicacy and pale green lucency to forest verdure. Approximately two-thirds of island ferns are endemic (i.e. not found anywhere else in the world). In order to appreciate the richness of Hawaii's fern flora, we might note here that there are 100 species of ferns in the entire central and eastern North America. Hawaiians of old used ferns for eating, brewing into tea, weaving hats and concocting medicines.

WOODFERNS (*Dryopteris walli-chiana*) and strapferns adorn a mossy forest mantle.

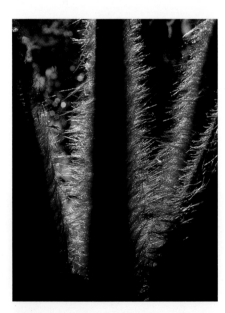

PULU, a densely scaled fluff from treefern stems, was formerly exported as pillow stuffing.

STRAP FERNS, or *ekaha (Elapho-glossum crassifolium)*, are common at lower elevations; some can be seen along the Hana Highway.

Forever replacing one another,
WOODFERN FIDDLEHEADS
unfurl their apple-green laciness
upwards and outwards, soon to turn
a darker shade of green.

The **HAIRY STRAP FERN** (*Elapho-glossum hirtum*) shows here a posture
which inspired its Greek name, "cow's
tongue."

FAIRYLANDS of mosses and ferns
add a special touch to Maui's high
elevation rain forests.

Water-soaked **FERNS GLISTEN** in the
shade of an unnamed waterfall at
5,000 feet in Waikamoi Preserve.

A close-up view of one of the super-hairy forest floor ferns in Waikamoi Preserve.

The silvery undersides of the common **HAPU'U**, a treefern *(Cibotium glaucum)*, make this an easy species to identify.

Hawaii's native **CAT'S CLAW CREEPER** *(Smilax sandwicensis)* has, during thousands of years of isolation from its mainland relatives, lost its spines. Here, it crawls across a *hapu'u* frond.

The bronze pigmentation of young **AMA'UMA'U FERN** *(Sadleria cyatheoides)* fronds protects young tissues from harmful light rays, acting like a sunscreen.

PIG STORY

Visitors and residents alike often ask why the water flowing over the Hana Highway's abundant waterfalls is so muddy, and whether it is safe to drink. Unfortunately, such sedimentation is largely unnatural; water should not be imbibed without treatment. Haleakala's wet forests, all the way from the Hana Highway up to the National Park's timberline, are overrun by large populations of feral pigs, whose browsing and "rototilling" activities, combined with Haleakala's steep slopes and abundant rainfall, cause extensive damage to Maui's watersheds. Under pristine conditions, the entire watershed was protected by a thick carpet of mosses growing from a rich layer of humus. This living sponge captured, then slowly released, enormous amounts of rainwater, essentially creating a reservoir from one to two feet deep over many square miles. Its rich layer of topsoil was also a nutritional nursery for millions of forest seedlings. This fabric of life is now mostly ripped asunder, much already washed down to the sea. Such happenings destroy pristine forests, endangering birds and plants, produce muddy and irregular waters that tarnish the beauty of flowing streams, and generate conditions hazardous to human health. Maui's north slope rain forests provide domestic water supplies for East Maui communities.

Maui's abundant **WATERFALLS** shrink to trickles during droughts and rage turbid during heavy rains.

A complex system of **FLUMES,** ditches, tunnels and pipes, maintained by East Maui Irrigation Company, carries Maui's most precious resource to thirsty consumers.

Pigs damage much more than the mossy ground layer as they dig for worms and starchy roots. They feast on a large variety of native plants. Here, a **NATIVE LILY** *(Astelia)*

flowers on a mossy log, while elsewhere in the Koolau Forest Reserve, a less fortunate plant lies victim to a voracious appetite.

Picturesque **TREEFERNS** (left) are special favorites of pigs, who gut them, often knocking them over, in quest of starch (right). Hollow

"trunks" collect water, providing breeding pools for mosquitos which then carry diseases such as avian malaria to native birds.

What a thrill to encounter a patch of truly **VIRGIN** (untouched) **FOREST,** brimming with thick carpets of moss and dense vegetation (left)! Much of Haleakala's windward slope, although appearing lush and green from afar, is actually wasted (right).

During a single storm, East Wailuaiki Stream carried enough **FOREST DEBRIS** to the beach to form a pile 300 feet long, twelve feet wide and six feet deep. Such excessive loss of leaf litter and rich topsoil deprives the forest of the nutrients it needs to sustain future growth. Scientists recently measured losses of *one inch of topsoil every three months* from Haleakala's forests!

RATS, such as the introduced Polynesian rat *(Rattus exulans)* shown here, prey upon birds eggs and young, and also eat the seeds of numerous native plants. Some biologists suspect they played a major role in the extinction of many forest birds. Rat populations are extremely large in the rain forest.

Native to Asia, the **RED-BILLED LEIOTHRIX** *(Leiothrix lutea),* introduced into Hawaii in 1911, is now abundant in the rain forest. Subsisting on fruit and insects, this beautiful little bird unfortunately carries diseases that are fatal to native birds.

The characteristic, bright blue-green plant emerging from a forest clearing is **MARIJUANA** (locally *pakalolo),* an enormously lucrative and illegal cash crop in the islands. It is said that pot brings in more money to the state than tourists! Who really knows, as most of it is grown illegally on state lands. This activity threatens violence to hikers and creates ideal conditions for aggressive weeds to spread into the forest; many weed seeds are inadvertently carried on growers' boots.

CONSERVATION EFFORTS

An unknown number (dozens) of Hawaii's native birds, found nowhere else in the world, have become extinct. Twenty-nine more are endangered, close to extinction. Today, there are as many birds endangered in Hawaii as in all of North America. Kauai artist Cheryl Boynton addresses a sobering question in her painting **"WILL THEY SURVIVE?"**

Fragile island ecosystems, always containing a high percentage of plants and animals found nowhere else in the world, are particularly vulnerable to disturbance. Hawaii's natural resources have suffered drastic changes ever since Polynesian man set foot here around 400 A.D.

Attempts to correct major problems in Hawaii's forests began with reforestation efforts early this century (see Hosmer Grove, page 32). They were boosted by the creation of Hawaii National Park in 1916, including what would later become Haleakala National Park on Maui, and by stringent efforts to reduce the numbers of feral cattle, sheep and goats in the forest reserves in the 1920s and '30s. It is only in the last decade however, that large-scale programs have addressed the enormity of damage effected by feral mammals on

Maui. This awareness was influenced greatly by a six-year, statewide forest bird survey conducted by the U.S. Fish & Wildlife Service. Today, management programs are mushrooming: The Nature Conservancy's Waikamoi Preserve, and a 37-mile mammal-proof fence encircling Haleakala National Park, both costing millions of dollars, attest to recent conservation endeavors. Hawaii's Senator Daniel Inouye lobbied hard to obtain funds to fence and manage Kipahulu Valley. The State of Hawaii, East Maui Irrigation Company and larger landowners are all showing increasing interest in the plight of Maui's precious watersheds. (Hunting around the forest fringes barely dents pig populations.) With such commitment, Maui's imperiled ecosystems may yet survive to enrich the lives of those who follow us.

Strong forces are at work attempting to reverse centuries of abuse in Maui's forests. Here, Henry Little, an executive from The Nature Conservancy, pauses in one of Maui's most pristine spots, **HAIPUAENA GULCH**, loaded with floral specialties.

The **WAIKAMOI PRESERVE**, created from land owned by Haleakala Ranch, here halts abruptly at the ranch's pasture above Olinda.

WAIKAMOI PRESERVE (pron. why-kah-moy). Hope springs from this newly preserved (1983) 5,270-acre section of rain forest managed by The Nature Conservancy. The hill against the skyline is 8,900-foot Hanakauhi Peak, described in Chapter III.

The **FOREST FLOOR** can bounce back with proper care. Here in Waiamoi Preserve, a field of stag's tongue ferns *(Elaphoglossum wawrae)* thrives on a forest flat once seriously disturbed by mammals.

KIPAHULU VALLEY

Incredible Kipahulu Valley (pron. key-pah-hoo-loo), added to Haleakala National Park in 1969, extends the park to the sea at Oheo Gulch ("Seven Pools"). Its dripping lushness, unique jungly verdure, magnificent waterfalls and unscalable precipices are rigorously protected by the park as a special scientific reserve. Access from the crater is prohibited. To reach the lower edges of this prime area of Maui, lavishly endowed with beauty, you must travel along the Hana Highway, Route 31. An entire chapter is devoted to it in *Maui's Hana Highway: A Visitor's Guide* by Angela Kay Kepler, which includes information on camping and trails.

MAKAHIKU FALLS, 185 feet high, can be reached by an easy twenty-minute hike from the Kipahulu campground.

KIPAHULU VALLEY from atop Puu Kuiki, above Paliku Cabin. The National Park now maintains hogwire fences throughout this rugged terrain.

A familiar landmark to all travelers on the road to Kipahulu, beautiful **WAILUA FALLS** thunders beside the roadside, framed by breadfruit and *kukui* trees.

Unrelenting water carves canyons of unending variety and beauty throughout the islands. Kipahulu's lower **OHEO GULCH** (left) exemplifies aqueous forces at work throughout Haleakala's wet forested slopes.

The dirt road beyond Kipahulu skirts the **WAVE-WORN CLIFFS** of East Maui's oldest lava as it passes between the younger lava flows at Kipahulu and Kaupo.

VII. SPECIAL AREAS

East Maui's seldom-seen **GREENSWORDS** *(Argyroxiphium virescens)*, close kin of the famous crater silverswords, favor waterlogged bogs where the sun rarely shines. They thrive in that dense blanket of grayness that you nearly always see as you look up at the mountains from Nahiku, Hana or Kipahulu.

Staggering contrasts are concentrated within the relatively small area that is Haleakala. Stony deserts and jagged lava vie with precipitous cliffs, hidden waterfalls, plunge pools, vistas of distant snow-capped peaks and riotously colored volcanic cinder cones. This geological diversity is carpeted with life zones ranging from alpine shrublands and barren lava flows of extreme aridity to sodden forests perpetually drenched by rivers of clouds. Skirting their broader areas, or hidden deeply within their confines, are postage stamp ecosystems which harbor exquisite plants: bogs, alpine lakes, belts of treeferns and grassy ridges. Merely realizing the existence of these floral treasures enhances our appreciation of Haleakala National Park and its adjacent forest reserves.

Delicate pink blossoms of a **BOG MINT** *(Phyllostegia ambigua)*, unique to Haleakala's alpine bogs, almost always have watersoaked tissues.

STORM CLOUDS swirl above eastern Haleakala — so many shades of clear gray! Such beauty continually recharges the forests and bogs with life-sustaining moisture.

RAINBOWS frequently grace Haleakala's cloud-swept slopes (above). Right at this elevation, around 7,000 feet, a narrow band of dwarf treeferns, **AMA'UMA'U** *(Sadleria cyatheoides)*, join rain forest with alpine shrubland in an eternal leafy embrace (left).

Thick carpets of native grassland *(Deschampsia australis)* cover the gently sloping alpine expanses above the forest. Here on **KALAPAWILI RIDGE,** 7,500 feet, grassy tussocks bask in some momentary sunshine ʾbefore enduring a prolonged bout of pouring rain.

Lakes, extremely rare in Hawaii, tend to be tucked away in unlikely places. Two lie huddled within forest-clad cinder cones close to upper Kipahulu Valley. **LAKE WAIANAPANAPA** ("glistening waters") — not to be confused with Waianapanapa coastal park near Hana — partially fills its cone with cold, sterile waters (left). Clouds normally conceal its presence, parting infrequently to provide a rare glimpse of its raspberry-ringed shore framed by a **"WHITE RAINBOW"** arching across its aeolian mists (right).

Remote, concealed, aloof...**LAKE WAIELEELE** ("waters with the color of Hawaiian eyes") peers darkly through a dense mantle of *'ohi'a*. These lakes harbor no fish and very few forms of aquatic life.

Finding a foothold in slightly raised ground, a **LONE 'OHI'A** tree invades the swampy domain of Maui's bog inhabitants.

Hidden high above Hana in the midst of forest-clad cinder cones lies Haleakala's largest, seldom-seen, **ALPINE BOG.**

Amorphous **MATS OF SHINING SILVER** dot Haleakala's bogs (left) which, on closer examination (right), are sprinkled with delicate geranium blossoms *(Geranium cuneatum)*. Although the same species as in the park's alpine shrubland (page 35), the plants here are stunted because of perpetually mushy soils, annual rainfall of over 400 inches and ephemeral sunshine.

"**GREENSWORD BOG**," now fenced for protection from pigs, houses the largest number of these fabulous plants in the world. After a variable number of years, each sends up a fast-growing shoot which develops into a showy cluster of more than 100 yellow "daisies."

Up until 1972, this species of **GREENSWORD** *(Argyroxiphium virescens)*, unique to Haleakala, was thought extinct except for one plant growing in cultivation. Note how its leafy rosette, similar to that of the silversword, is far less silvery.

Though smaller than its desert counterpart, a **FLOWERING GREENSWORD** never fails to excite scientists who trudged through many thousands of feet of elevation for three days to reach its isolated habitat.

Majestically arising from water-sodden bogs (left), the **PU'E** *(Lobelia gaudichaudii)* sprouts an enormous cluster of curved, purple-and-white flowers (right).

Like nothing else you've ever seen, the most spectacular plant of the entire mountain, except perhaps the silversword, is the **KOLI'I** *(Tremato-lobelia macrostachys)* which adorns the edges of mist shrouded bogs with its long, radiating arms (left) jam-packed with cerise flowers (right). Unique to the islands, this is another example of Hawaii's precious natural heritage.

ABOUT THE AUTHORS

Cameron Kepler

Angela Kay Kepler

Cameron and Kay Kepler met in Honolulu in 1964 while Kay was an East-West Center foreign student and Cameron was studying Pacific seabirds for the U.S. National Museum. They have worked together as a biological team since their marriage in Honolulu in 1966. Kay, a naturalized New Zealander, was born in Australia in 1943, while Cameron, born in 1938, hails from California. Both earned Ph.D. degrees in vertebrate zoology at Cornell University, New York, Kay receiving degrees en route from the University of Canterbury, New Zealand, and the University of Hawaii, Honolulu, while Cam completed degrees at the University of California, Santa Barbara, in English literature and zoology. In 1972, they spent a year at Oxford University, England, as visiting researchers. Over the past two decades, they have authored or co-authored twelve books, more than 60 scientific publications and numerous technical reports. Kay has also written newspaper columns and magazine articles specializing in biological aspects of the Hawaiian Islands. Cam is an endangered species field biologist with the U.S. Fish and Wildlife Service. Together, the Keplers have conducted forest bird and plant surveys, seabird studies and endangered species research in the mainland U.S., Hawaii, West Indies and New Zealand. They have hiked, camped, worked and canoed throughout Hawaii's mountains, lowlands and coastlines.

The Kepler family includes two adopted daughters, Sylvelin and Leilani (p. 24, bottom photo, center and right).

FRONT COVER: Crumbly lava cliffs tumble into Haleakala Crater at Koolau Gap (note hiker at lower right).

BACK COVER: A dazzling native 'I'iwi *(Vestiaria coccinea)* sips nectar from the spectacular, multi-rayed koli'i *(Trematolobelia macrostachys),* high in Haleakala's native rain forests.